NEBRASKA POETRY

A Sesquicentennial Anthology
1867–2017

NEBRASKA STATEHOOD 1867 2017 150

A Legacy Project of the Nebraska 150 Celebration

NEBRASKA POETRY

A Sesquicentennial Anthology
1867–2017

Edited by Daniel Simon

STEPHEN F. AUSTIN STATE UNIVERSITY PRESS
2017

To all my teachers
To all my students
To all Nebraskans

Publication of this book was made possible in part by generous support from the Dr. C. C. & Mabel L. Criss Library, University of Nebraska Omaha, the UNO Library Friends, and the Center for Great Plains Studies, University of Nebraska–Lincoln.

Royalties from the first edition will be donated to the Jane Pope Geske Heritage Room of Nebraska Authors, Lincoln City Libraries.

Manufactured in Korea

ISBN 978-1-62288-145-1

For more information:
Stephen F. Austin State University Press
P.O. Box 13007 SFA Station
Nacogdoches, Texas 75962
sfapress@sfasu.edu
www.sfasu.edu/sfapress
936-468-1078

Book Design: Kimberly Verhines
Cover Photo: Michael Forsberg

Before my dead eyes open, flooding me with nothing,
let me speak to you of the few remaining pods
of the catalpa trees now hung with snow.
What are they if not old flutes against a background
of untroubled white, instruments to play the heart to?
– Don Welch, "L'Envoi," from *A Day Book*

At dusk your flight
signals that we are close,
almost there,
or should be gone.
– Nancy McCleery, "Everything Keeps Me Here, the Swallow"

Contents

Foreword

by Twyla M. Hansen

Nebraska has long held its historic authors in high regard, with groups, centers, and scholarship devoted to Willa Cather, John Neihardt, Mari Sandoz, Loren Eiseley, Bess Streeter Aldrich, Wright Morris, and other prominent fiction/nonfiction writers. But it was poetry writing that in 1921 motivated Nebraska to legislate an official position and to unanimously appoint Neihardt—a decade before his *Black Elk Speaks* fame—as our poet laureate. Almost one hundred years later, I'm pleased to report that poetry is alive and thriving in Nebraska.

The word *poem* comes from a Greek word meaning "to make." Like all the arts, poems have been made by all cultures—written or handed down in the oral tradition through songs, prayers, and stories—to preserve what was important to people in their time. Nebraska's former state poet, William Kloefkorn, acknowledged the worth of writing poetry when he defined a poem as "words, highly distilled, nibbling at the edge of something vast."

In *Nebraska Poetry: A Sesquicentennial Anthology,* editor Daniel Simon has collected poems that indeed nibble at that vastness. This is Nebraska's most comprehensive and well-researched poetry anthology to date, inclusive of gender, age, ethnicity, and geographic areas of the state. The poems range from the settling of the West, to reflections of a past/agrarian lifestyle, to nature/environment, to the more urban poems of the twenty-first century. The poets and their work are arranged by year of birth, which allows us to appreciate the change of styles and subjects that have always occurred in poetry as well as the continuum of similarities. This volume is a delight to peruse and offers readers the rare opportunity to discover so many voices—the almost-forgotten women writing in the early 1900s to those in the present generation. Most of the contributors are contemporary poets writing at the height of their careers.

Poetry is a big tent with room for all kinds. Most poems in *Nebraska Poetry* are Great Plains-centered, with its wide-open expanses, but are not limited in scope or experience or geographic borders. There is a plethora of styles and subjects in the anthology, and inventive uses of form—sonnets, rhyme, meter, blank verse, and more, but mostly *vers libre*, with dazzling examples of metaphor, diction, and syntax.

On the Great Plains, the weather is a big deal and is used often in these poems. The Dust Bowl of the 1930s lives again in poems by Don Welch ("When Memory Gives Dust a Face") and Allison Hedge Coke ("Then"). Tornadoes and thunderstorms crash about, and wind sweeps the land clean with heat, drought, and hail. Water is plentiful here in the form of rain, pond, river, and stream and is sucked up from underground to spread on crops. The sky can be filled with ominous clouds; away from city lights, the night sky reveals its bowl of twinkling stars.

Place is often used as a character or background, as lonesome or populated; it is memorialized, celebrated, and scorned. Love is ever-present in most of these poems, many through family relationships. Community is here, as are war, sex, and politics. Loss is evident through poems of despair, destruction, and/or death. Nature is sometimes used as a backdrop reflecting our own human emotions. Humor is here, too, mostly the dry-wit sort and often with a sharp edge.

There are also echoes in the anthology across time and subject. Two examples are "The Death of Crazy Horse" by Neihardt and the earth-centered song lyrics in "Crazy Horse" by contemporary indigenous writer John Trudell; and the call of Kees's mid-twentieth-century "For My Daughter" and its response by contemporary poet Grace Bauer in "Note from the Imaginary Daughter."

This is an anthology I will return to often for insight and inspiration; it warms me to read so many poems I wish I had written. The memorable poems go well beyond the words, ending sometimes in ambiguity, allowing the reader to appreciate and interpret them. What I notice above all is how the poets here have honored the essential life force of poetry: the act of paying close attention. The ordinary world of this time and this place—in the right hands and with the right words—becomes extraordinary.

In so many ways, *Nebraska Poetry* is a historic record of our state as reflected through the hearts and minds of its poets. Editor Simon has added to the literary history of Nebraska with this publication. It will serve our state well through the years as a resource for teachers, students, writers, historians, and researchers as well as for the general public. The anthology is a creative glimpse into Nebraska's past and present, and it bodes well for our poetic future. Let us go forth and celebrate 150 years of Nebraska statehood and its wide-sky tent filled with poetry!

Lincoln, Nebraska
Nebraska State Poet, 2013–2018

Introduction: 150 Years of Nebraska Poetry
by Daniel Simon

> *There are without doubt new writers rising out of the Plains, . . . but where is the writer with the gusto, the wild immeasurable power, the wide horizons, the sense of the universal in man, and his infinite variety?*
> – Mari Sandoz, *Love Song to the Plains* (1961)

In his *Semi-centennial History of Nebraska* (1904), Addison E. Sheldon compared the state's history to "a great book of stone and clay and dirt whose story will be read with increasing interest through the years as our power to translate it grows." During 150 years of statehood, Nebraska's poets have occupied a first rank among those who would read—and write—that book of stone, clay, and dirt, anchoring their work in "the great fact of the land itself," in Willa Cather's apt phrase. Nebraska's position at a geographical crossroads, according to Sheldon, makes the state "the heart of the continent, the pathway of Empire." Sheldon, who homesteaded in the Sandhills of Cherry County in the 1880s, served in the Nebraska House of Representatives in the 1890s, and later became superintendent of the Nebraska State Historical Society between the world wars, took on the role of cultural impresario for the young state in his next book, the illustrated *Poems and Sketches of Nebraska* (1908). "The material for a new literature is here," he wrote, sounding one of the great themes of Nebraska writers in the new century. Their task was to make a "new literature" out of whatever materials they had brought with them or could unearth—or otherwise appropriate—in the landscape they now occupied.

Writing a century after Lewis and Clark made their way up the Missouri River, Sheldon lionized the pioneers in his poetic sketches, which are marked by a boosterish strain that characterizes much of the early poetry published in and about the state. Such boosterism—and utopianism—inspired countless poems that extoll the state's natural beauty. "For lo, the light breaks over the plains," a line by Melisse LePoste, typifies such enthusiasm. In a similar vein, Frederick Blaine Humphrey exalts the pioneers' ability to "harmonize with the great law of progressive growth" in his preface to *Poems by Nebraska Poets*: "Here is no place for the idler," he writes. "This is a country for red-blooded men and women, for the strong, the ambitious. . . . Nebraska is the home of the virile" (vol. 2, 1941).

That sense of heroic exceptionalism remains rooted in the state's psyche today. The first known anthology, *Nebraska Poets*, coincided with the 1898 Trans-Mississippi Exposition in Omaha. Edited by Carl Smith, the managing editor of the *Omaha World-Herald*, the handsome anthology, with its elegant navy blue cover, clearly aimed to showcase the state's nascent literary culture to the exposition's 2.6 million visitors: Smith's boss, William Jennings Bryan, had served as the *World-Herald's* editor in chief prior to his first presidential run in 1896. (Bryan's successor at the newspaper, Richard Lee Metcalfe, published a campaign biography about the "fearless and brilliant" orator.) Although many of the poems in Smith's anthology haven't aged well, Lucy Martin Bullock's "Decoration Day" *(featured here on page 37)* is typical of the patriotic tributes that became popular, in the years following the Civil War, to the Union and Confederate dead. More than three thousand men from the Nebraska Territory had fought in the ranks of the Union Army, and thousands more would serve in the Spanish-American War and the wars to come in the twentieth and twenty-first centuries.

Although the first anthology had its roots in Omaha, by the early twentieth century much of the literary energy of the state shifted to Lincoln, home to the University of Nebraska. Beginning with the appointment of poet Orasmus Charles Dake as the first professor of English literature at the university in 1871, a succession of professors that included Prosser Hall Frye and Herbert Bates nurtured the likes of Edwin Ford Piper, Louise Pound, Willa Cather, Hartley Burr Alexander, Margaret Haughawout, Mari Sandoz, Ione Gardner, Clarissa Bucklin, Helene Magaret, Loren Eiseley, Bernice Slote, and Weldon Kees (all featured in the present anthology, with the exception of Pound and Sandoz). Many students at the university cut their teeth as poets in *The Mid-West Quarterly,* which Frye edited from 1913 to 1918, or in *Prairie Schooner*, founded in 1926. When the Great Depression hit in 1929, several students or former students of Lowry Charles Wimberly, a professor of English and *Prairie Schooner's* founding editor (1926–56), helped make the Federal Writers' Project state guidebook one of the best books in the series—after working on *Nebraska: A Guide to the Cornhusker State* (1939), Loren Eiseley, Weldon Kees, and Mari Sandoz would go on to brilliant careers in the years following the Second World War.

A few years earlier, writing in *The Nation* in 1923, Willa Cather had struck an elegiac tone about her adopted state, characterizing it as a "highway for dreamers and adventurers" that "led out, but never back again" ("Nebraska: The End of the First Cycle"). For Cather, writers belonging to what she called "the third generation" following the pioneers faced the task of "breaking the hard molds of provincialism." Such provincialism—characteristic of the poetry included here by Dake, Bullock, Piper, Cather, Jarvis, Slote, and even, to some extent, Neihardt—began showing cracks in its façade by the 1920s as a number of the university-trained poets set about writing poetry that shared many of the hallmarks of literary modernism. Beginning with Margaret Haughawout, Ione Gardner, Clarissa Bucklin, and especially Helene Magaret, female poets also began chafing at the conventions, both social and literary, imposed by their (mostly older, mostly male) professors and peers. In her poem "Song of the Answerer," Magaret, after having worked as a foreign correspondent and translator in Spain in the 1920s, parodies Whitman's nativism while at the same time offering a scathing indictment of Depression-era America (*page 60*). In "Come Out of the Cold," she warns of a "wind called War, and its black flame" that, by 1941, threatened to "Wither the world." A young Tillie Olsen—already a champion of labor, social, and political causes in her late teens and early twenties—also sounds a defiant note in "I Want You Women up North to Know" (*page 69*), addressed to northern society ladies who purchased dresses "dyed in blood . . . stitched in wasting flesh" by seamstresses in the South. Olsen wrote the poem a few weeks before being arrested, at the age of twenty-two, during the West Coast waterfront strike of 1934.

In the postwar era, Weldon Kees would strike the most modern pose of all the Nebraska modernists in three verse collections—*The Last Man* (1943), *The Fall of the Magicians* (1947), and *Poems 1947–1954* (1954)—although his posthumous reputation didn't achieve critical mass until the 1980s. James A. Emanuel, in poems like "Negritude" and "Black Poet on the Firing Range" as well as scholarly essays and his anthology *Dark Symphony: Negro Literature in America* (1968), is a key figure in bridging the Harlem Renaissance of Langston Hughes, Zora Neale Hurston, and Ralph Ellison with the African American writers who flourished in the 1950s, '60s, and '70s. Although Kees and Emanuel were both born in Nebraska (in Beatrice and Alliance, respectively), their best-known works and literary legacies were achieved outside the state. Another "outsider," Karl Shapiro, took over the editorship of *Prairie Schooner* from Wimberly in 1956 but resigned in 1963 after taking umbrage when a university dean censored (on grounds of obscenity) a story by Nebraska native Ervin Krause.

By the late 1960s and early 1970s, a flourishing scene of little magazines and small presses centered in Lincoln, Kearney, and Omaha empowered poets in the state to achieve an autonomous publishing economy marked by a strong regionalist character that, for the most part, avoided the traps of provincialism. "The emergence was heralded by a stunned director of the National Endowment for the Arts speaking at a national meeting," recalled Don Welch. "It was as if some giant poetic egg was hatching in Nebraska."* Following the national renown achieved from the 1920s to the 1950s by the writers of Nebraska's first literary renaissance—chiefly Willa Cather, Bess Streeter Aldrich, John G. Neihardt, Mari Sandoz, and Wright Morris†—this second renaissance was led by a vanguard of

* National Endowment for the Arts literature director Len Randolph took note of Nebraska's poetry renaissance at a national meeting in the early 1970s; Welch's comments on the "poetic egg" are found in Hawkins and Fisher-Vrana, *Alive and Writing in Nebraska* (1986). Dana Gioia helpfully distinguishes between provincialism and regionalism in his essay on Ted Kooser, "The Anonymity of the Regional Poet" (1983), reprinted in *The Sandhills Reader*.

† See Donald R. Hickey, Susan A. Wunder, and John R. Wunder, "Willa Cather and Her Pulitzer Prize," "The Pound Family," and "Nebraska's Literary Renaissance," in *Nebraska Moments* (new ed., 2007). Eiseley is included in the chapter on "Nebraska's Scientists."

poets alongside such fiction and nonfiction writers as Kent Haruf, Jonis Agee, David Wiltse, Mary Pipher, and Ron Hansen. The important poets whose work began appearing in the 1970s and '80s included William Kloefkorn, Don Welch, Nancy McCleery, Shirley Buettner, Hilda Raz, Ted Kooser, and Greg Kuzma. As professors, editors, and/or publishers of creative writing—in addition to being major poets in their own right—Kloefkorn, Welch, Raz, Kooser, and Kuzma have had an immeasurable impact on subsequent generations of Nebraska poets, as have Greg Kosmicki, JV Brummels, Art Homer, and Mark Sanders in more recent years.*

In many respects, the genealogy of Nebraska poetry can be traced as a nearly unbroken succession of teachers and their students whose work has found encouragement on the many college and university campuses around the state, from Orasmus Charles Dake and his students in the 1870s to the youngest poet featured here, Kelly Weber, who dedicates her poem "Mentor" to JV Brummels. That strong mentoring relationship—and a persistent intergenerational faith in teaching the craft of writing—has fostered an exceptionally close-knit and supportive literary community around the state that will no doubt extend its reach well into the twenty-first century.

What makes a "Nebraska" poem, then? It must be noted that the poems published in the state from 1867 onward arose within the broader history and literary landscape of the Great Plains, amidst "the oral literatures of the many Native nations who have lived in the area and with the folktales and dramas of the early European and mixed-blood peoples" (*Encyclopedia of the Great Plains*). Nebraska's print culture in many ways drew from the oral and pictorial traditions native to the region while at the same time effacing large swaths of the peoples and cultures that gave rise to them. On the new *Poetry from the Plains* website, Stephen Behrendt helpfully situates the rise of Nebraska's literature against "the pattern of predominantly east–west postcolonial human transit," which "overlaid an extant, ancient north–south axis that had been inscribed for countless centuries by the migratory patterns of native creatures like the bison, sandhill cranes, and snow geese whose astonishing numbers were decimated by the human interventions that pushed such native creatures to the brink of extinction" ("Some Preliminary Notes on Nebraska, Poetry, and Nebraska Poetry"). From Loren Eiseley to Kathleene West, many Nebraska poets—including Native poets Donna Whitewing, John Trudell, Laura Tohe, and Allison Hedge Coke—are haunted by the losses that exist just below the surface and along the side roads of Sheldon's "pathway of Empire."

* Some of the small presses that came of age during the second renaissance and in more recent years include Abattoir/Penumbra, Backwaters, Best Cellar, Blue Heron, Gibraltar, Logan House, Lone Willow, Platte Valley, Sandhills, Slow Tempo, Three Sheets, and Windflower.

The question of what makes a poem a "Nebraska" poem remains. (More on my definition of "Nebraska" writers in a moment.) It's a question I posed to each of the living writers whose work makes up the greater share of *Nebraska Poetry*; some of their responses are included as mini-epigraphs below. In the following section I'd like to focus on four broad themes—*land, time, language*, and *community*—that, to my mind, begin to answer that question.* While it seemed best to organize the anthology chronologically, the distinctiveness of Nebraska poetry emerges from the poems themselves, which converse with one another in ways that disrupt linear chronologies.

1. Land

> *Nebraska literature is so firmly rooted in the landscape to begin with. There's a certain sensibility that comes from that perspective—literally, from the ground up. Makes for an aesthetic that's direct, open, simple (though not simplistic), and often tough. Through time, Nebraska and Nebraskans have become a mosaic of sensibilities, cultures, dreams, and aspirations.* – Kathleen Cain

Beginning with the land, Nebraska poets inscribe their work in the age-old nature/culture dyad, the modern version of which was bequeathed to Western culture by the Romantics. The high plains were hardly a blank slate, however: Paleo-Indians and Plains-Woodland peoples have inhabited the area since at least 10,000 B.C.E. In more recent centuries, the land that became Nebraska has been sacred geography to many generations of Native inhabitants, including the Pawnee, Ponca, Otoe-Missouria, Omaha, Lakota, Arapaho, Cheyenne, Santee (Eastern Dakota), and Winnebago nations. In his essay "Defining the Vernacular of Nebraska Poetry" (2011), Mark Sanders writes that the beauty of Nebraska "exists at the center of a space that should not be regarded as negative, where even absence is tangible. One of the advantages that Nebraska poets have is not just the language of the particular but the big empty that contains the particulars." That "big empty"—which Karl Shapiro, with a mix of affection and irony, calls "Nowhere"—starts with the land beneath poets' feet, seeps into bodies and minds, and is projected onto blank pages that mirror the vast skies over their heads. Amy Plettner writes of "April's deafening pitch" (*page 236*), acknowledging the sheer abundance of life-forms and ecoregions that surround and, at times, threaten to overwhelm the writer. Yet against the backdrop of this "state made all of sky," the pioneer who builds a sod house in Erin Belieu's "Plainsong" finds "a shape to love" in the contours of a woman wearing a brown dress and to whom, in marriage, he would give his "grass soul" (*page 242*).

* Robert Brooke, director of the Nebraska Writing Project, identifies five themes: heritage, landscape, imagination, social action, and humor (Cox and MacDaniels, *Guide to Nebraska Authors*, 1998).

Many of Nebraska's most famous writers, including Cather, Neihardt, and Kooser, were not born within its borders but, in time, brought an outsider's perspective to bear on what makes the state unique. Charles Fort felt like he had landed in "imaginative exile" when he first came to the state: "I reconnected from the strange and beautiful landscape of the Great Plains to the other interior places of my life through memory and imagination" (personal email). To some writers, the prairie evokes terror or ennui, but a poet like Ted Kooser learns to take comfort and delight in the call of a screech owl that "with small hope / from the center of darkness / . . . calls out again and again" (*page 108*).

Not only the land and its life-forms but the state's waterways make their presence felt in these pages. Filled with solicitude for water's scarcity, poets from river towns like Crawford, Ogallala, Ord, and Plattsmouth find in water a constant wellspring of inspiration in a state where memories of the Dust Bowl still loom large. Mark Sanders calls water on the plains "the great wheel turning," with the human presence standing at its center. For Diné poet Laura Tohe, the Platte River is a "singing miracle," invoking in her bilingual poem the song of the cranes, geese, and other bird species that use the state's rivers, lakes, and streams as compass points and places of rest and refuge (*page 204*). In a compilation of articles originally published as newspaper columns on the occasion of Nebraska's 125th anniversary, Paul Johnsgard called the Platte "the very lifeblood symbol of Nebraska." Moreover, he wrote, the "angelic voices" of the sandhill cranes "capture the very essence and spirit of our state" (*Nebraska Voices*). Looking at Mike Forsberg's photograph on the book's cover, the feather almost dances before your eyes. For many of the poets featured here, the cranes represent a spirit of creation as old as the land itself.

Of course, the open plains are not the only landscapes depicted in poetry by Nebraskans: the state's cities and towns frequently appear in the following pages, including the Omaha of William Trowbridge and Michael Catherwood, the Lincoln of William Kloefkorn and Twyla Hansen, as well as the hundreds of small towns that poets usually try to escape from before returning, in memory and the imagination, to write about the formative years they spent there. For Weldon Kees, his hometown of Beatrice in a poem like "1926" is as much a landscape of the mind as it is an actual place, "mapped and marred" in memory.

For students and scholars seeking to understand how place influences literature, the present anthology offers a rich and diverse case study upon which to base their analyses.

2. Time

> *I think a Nebraska poem is one written with that state's presence as a ground, as in music, for the language. First the light, then the horizon, then the history of the Great Plains, then the literary riches of our Nebraska progenitors built in me, over decades, a sense of belonging to Nebraska's multiplicity of identities and ambitions.* – Hilda Raz

Of all the writers featured in *Nebraska Poets*, Loren Eiseley is most deeply attuned to the millennial cycles of natural history. Calling his work "the poems of a bone hunter and a naturalist," Eiseley reads the book of the land as much for its mutability as for its enduring presence, as interested in how "one culture tumbles into another" as in the artifacts any single culture might leave behind. Writing in "The High Plains" about his discovery of the pink catlinite bowl of an Indian pipe during the 1930s, he sees how debris sifts down onto the hardpan and concludes: "Looking on there one saw everything, including one's self, in final perspective. / Five hundred human generations / leave very little. / On the high plains / the soft stuff goes first / and that includes / man" (*page 64*).

Such historicized knowledge—set as it is against a landscape that can be as forbidding as it is fecund—seems to obsess Nebraska poets, often taking the form of creation myths, from birth stories to acts of artistic imagination. For Willa Cather, the "fierce necessity" and "sharp desire" of Youth sings "out of the lips of silence" (*page 44*). In William Kloefkorn's "My Love for All Things Warm and Breathing" (a canonical Nebraska poem if there ever was one), the "boundless lust" of all things gathers force from the students in his classroom "to scatter it fine and / enormous into the trees and the grass, into the heat / beneath the earth beneath the stone" (*page 83*). For Greg Kuzma, the humble act of planting a tree signifies not only an appreciation for natural beauty but a leap of faith across generations. In a state that remains largely rural, the cycle of the seasons is marked by the rituals of planting and harvesting, what Ben Gotschall calls "taking and taking care." And Kassandra Montag writes of "desire itself," buffeted by a "bitter wind [that] flails from the north" (*page 280*). The poet's keen attention to the moment-by-moment changes happening around her remains grounded in a deeper appreciation for the cyclical nature of time.

Just as common as creation myths, death haunts these pages as well. From the child-sized graves in poems by Dake and West; to Piper and Neihardt writing about the slaughter of bison and the murder of Crazy Horse in the 1870s; to burial scenes in Behrendt, Fort, and Harrison; to poems about violent death by Holland, Raz, Deal, Black, Waggener, Black, and McKinstry-Brown—what might seem like a land of mythic eternal return is just as often punctuated by the stark moments of mortality that attend life on the prairies, portents that loom large like the loaded gun under the pickup seat in Sam Renken's "The Price of Hay's Gone Up Terribly." In "Nebraska" *(page 234)*, Kelly Madigan writes:

> This is a place for things that take time, the long stitching together
> of soft spots in the heart, the wind across the Missouri River Valley
> scooping loess into hills unlike any others on this continent,
> seeds stored in the cellar of the prairie for a hundred years
> patient for fire, unable to crack themselves open without it.
> This is a place where disappointments deep as aquifer
> can spill themselves out, fill up and empty again, as many times
> as the wound requires. This is a place where a person can heal,
> or choose not to heal. We have both kinds.

Things that take time. Faced with a sense of place and time that can both comfort and overwhelm, Nebraska poets have forged a literature that, over decades, provides a "sense of belonging to Nebraska's multiplicity of identities and ambitions" (Raz).

3. Language

> *What do I think makes a "Nebraska" poem? There is a certain character of voice—unafraid to be colloquial, bighearted, sometimes modest, sometimes making claims large as the Plains itself, generous in spirit.* – Judith Sornberger

Against the backdrops of nature and history, culture emerges, in a literary sense, most dramatically as a preoccupation with language. In Susan Aizenberg's "Georgic on Waking," the speaker's eye roves over an edenic panorama of emergent consciousness as darkness gives way to light: "Then speak that language / you knew before you knew language, / before you had to learn day's difficult / vocabulary, that yammering patois" (*page 183*). For many of the poets included here, although an escapist nostalgia for a purer, private language is a constant theme, our shared, public, "yammering patois" is where some of the state's best poems begin.

For me, one of the most moving poems featured in *Nebraska Poetry* is Don Welch's "Requiem for a Teacher" (*page 88*), which begins:

> Not everyone can be informed by love,
> nor every word worn and measured by grief's tongue.
> In loss the shoulders of the blackbirds are our sum.

Yet if flight is song,
the cranes will come again to tell us what wing is,
and canaries bless our cottonwoods.

This beloved teacher, having given his very "bones' chalk," leads students "to the edge, and just beyond" of knowledge. As is so often the case in these pages, song arises out of "grief's tongue." Welch, himself the student here, observes that his teacher's "shadow, smokeless, stays upon our tongues." From one-room schoolhouses to campus classrooms, many Nebraska poets take inspiration from teachers who convey their passion for making languages sing.

In his "Defining the Vernacular" essay, Mark Sanders makes a case for finding pleasure—and poetry—in the "spoken cadences" of everyday speech. And in a manifesto of sorts that illustrates his thesis, his poem "Plain Sense" advocates "Plain speech for a plain people: / weather-words gray as old lumber; / old sheds and old houses / sitting on the tilted legs of wind" (*page 216*). Yet even plain speech requires familiarity with the codes and local nuances that give words meaning, as in Hilda Raz's "Diction." And from the spoken language, writers turn to written forms to give a sense of permanence to the evanescence of speech. In Matt Mason's "Pencils (At the Nebraska State Juvenile Detention Center)," following the speaker's initial observation of the "haiku on the dry-erase board" that keep track of the pencils given to the detainees, he discovers that after breaking off the tips, "they will wrap toilet paper tight / to hold the nub, / to scratch stories and poems, / small knife disappearing / into words they write" (*page 250*). In many of Nebraska's greatest poems, colloquial language mixes with traditional forms—sonnets, villanelles, pantoums, elegies, rondels, and more—to create moments of lasting literary value.

If place and time are the "great facts" of existence, language enables writers to "press back against the pressure of reality," as Wallace Stevens once wrote, in times of peace or war, fecundity or drought, bliss or despair ("The Noble Rider and the Sound of Words"). What Helene Magaret calls "the roaring chaos" just outside the door inspires Nebraska poets with a fierce desire to press back against whatever existential threats might silence or imperil them.

4. Community

Why do you keep imagining me in other places and states?
And why do you keep assuming our children are unhappy?
– Don Welch, "Nebraska"

Out of a patchwork of geographies, histories, and tongues, Nebraska poets delight in creating a cultural tapestry that shows its seams and imperfections while also covering the state like a familiar quilt. In his "Nebraska" poem cited above, Don Welch imagines the state as a Russian woman having "a certain large-boned beauty about her" who might be "a pawn in huge novels of war" (*page 87*). The society in microcosm depicted in the following pages reflects much of the social fabric of the state.

Many of the poems here sketch tableaux of society in miniature: the one-on-one relationships of couples, parents and their children, and siblings. In "Prairie Poem with Lines from Emily Dickinson" (*page 239*), Steve Langan imagines a dialogue that might have taken place between homesteaders in the 1860s just as easily as it could be spoken by a working-class couple today as they decide whether to "pull up stakes" or remain in a place they may or may not find hospitable:

> Let's live here forever – this broken wavering
> spell – but only if you promise to say,
>
> "Only through the grace of one crazed
> and simple plan" when someone asks,
> "Did you really live there then?"
>
> And say – "I was happy there, almost glad."

Other poems intimate the darker relationships between neighbors, racial and ethnic groups, and competing interests of class and politics. Shirley Buettner writes about her rural neighbor, "framed" by the cornfield between them, who gradually disappears as the corn grows up between their houses. After the neighbor's windows "flare and wink" at the speaker of the poem in the second stanza, the neighbor, briefly seen hoeing corn, is completely swallowed up. Even her personified house—with its façade of mouth, nose, eyes, and hair—disappears, leaving only the wash on the clothesline "flap[ping] tearfully, / white handkerchiefs waving / goodbye, goodbye" (*page 96*). In another Buettner poem, the occupants of a township experience "a loosening, then a loss," a fate common to many communities where residents drift away, businesses and schools close, and the "soft stuff" of Eiseley's human presence on the plains disappears.

In other poems, communities that fade and fray around the edges find ways of making do together. Stepping onto the porch to shake the crumbs from his tablecloth, Greg Kosmicki imagines the cloth as a flag honored not by jingoistic patriotism but by communal sharing: "I want you to come and join me / and my family, I want you to sit // at my table and have bread and lasagna with us / so we can talk about the war and taxes." Gathered around a table, "I know you could not be a traitor to me," he writes: "we will all be so insanely happy // we had not yet had to die for any cause / I want you to spill your wine / I want you to get bread crumbs on my flag" (*page 161*). In choosing "My Flag" as one of her favorite Nebraska poems, Sarah McKinstry-Brown writes warmly of her fondness for Kosmicki's poem: "With every new election cycle or war or conflict, I find myself returning to this poem; it's a beautiful reminder of what the world might look like if we all dropped our flags, our ideologies, and gathered around a table to break bread" (personal email).

Around another table, Grace Bauer imagines a mealtime blessing that playfully pokes fun at clichés about the state's bland food, congeniality, conservatism, and resilience (what some might call stubbornness):

> Bless us, Oh Lord,
> and this our Jell-O. Our corn,
> our steaks and kolaches.
> . . . .
> Bless our perseverance.
> Our unerring politeness.
> Our red state politics
> and our white, white bread.
> Bless our dubious status
> as *tornado alley*, as *flyover zone*
> and bless all those who fly over,
> as well as those of us who, out of
> choice or necessity or inertia –
> forgive us, we know not why or what
> we've done – but, by God, stayed.
> ("Great Plains Prayer," page 196)

Communities gather in all shapes and sizes here: among Clarissa Bucklin's puritanical Ladies' Aid group, in the cathedral-like train stations of Lavon Jarvis, on the night trains of Karl Shapiro and Allison Hedge Coke, in the hospital rooms of William Kloefkorn's "three queens" (nurses) and Erik Campbell's dying father, at William Trowbridge's Peony Park, around Roy Scheele's racetrack, in Barbara Schmitz's backyard, on Lenora Castillo's "small farm in the middle of nowhere," in the black-and-white frames of Michael Catherwood's home movies and Alexander Payne's *Nebraska* (referred to in John Brehm's "Nebraska"), in Amy Plettner's Sunday-morning church, in the Dust Bowl schoolhouse and cemetery of Ted Genoways's ancestors, at Ben Gotschall's rodeo, and in Cat Dixon's church food pantry. Nebraskans know both the "blood price" (Hilda Raz) of tragedies that rip the social fabric in a poem like Sarah McKinstry-Brown's "After 13 Months of Searching, the Girl's Body Is Found Five Miles from Our House" as well as the healing to be found in Neil Harrison's "Spring Burial in the Sandhills."

Just as every sort of community can be found in these pages, the broader social makeup of the state is woven into its literary fabric as well. "There is a Nebraska poetry community," writes Sanders, "one that has grown up considerably over the past century and that has much connective tissue" ("Defining the Vernacular"). Part of that community derives from the generosity with which Nebraska poets read and nurture one another's work. In a call for papers that appears in a special issue of *Pebble* (1975) devoted to Nebraska verse, Greg Kuzma writes: "It is my very great interest right now to be able to say for myself what poems continue to hold me, and hear what others say about what they are reading and rereading, what has sustained them. What I propose is a book of essays on poems or books of poems that continue to matter."* That conversation continues today in coffee shops, classrooms, and kitchens all over the state and in programs like the UNL-sponsored Nebraska Writing Project, "a network of professional educators and affiliated writers [that] provides opportunities to improve, enhance, and celebrate writing for classrooms and communities across Nebraska"; the many projects supported by Humanities Nebraska and the Nebraska Arts Council; and Poetry Out Loud, which encourages high school students to memorize their favorite poems and then recite them in competitions at the local, state, and national levels. The most recent Poetry Out Loud anthology includes several of the poets featured in *Nebraska Poetry:* Weldon Kees, Karl Shapiro, Ted Kooser, Twyla Hansen, Allison Hedge Coke, and John Brehm.

If a poem is a snapshot capturing a moment in time and place, and a verse collection like a poet's album of photos, anthologies serve as mini-archives, gathering, in this case, a family of albums that reach across time to create word pictures of a place that we glimpse through the eyes of others as much as our own. Just as Susan Strayer Deal imagines the inhabitants of a sod house pulling out their upright piano to pose for a photograph (à la Solomon Butcher), the poets here all offer portraits of places and moments that might otherwise be lost to history.

Anthologies are also acts of *literary* history. Within American literature, Nebraska poetry reflects the broader trends that have characterized the past 150 years of U.S. literary history, yet it retains a distinctive plains ethos that distinguishes it

* Kuzma eventually published that book, *A Book of Rereadings in Recent American Poetry: 30 Essays*, with Best Cellar Press in 1979.

from the predominantly urban aesthetic of either coast. And while Nebraska's history has been masterfully told, for a state with such a rich and diverse literature now more than a century and a half old, our literary story remains to be gathered into a cohesive narrative. Galleries of the evolving poetic landscape exist, to be sure: the anthologies included in the "For Further Reading" list that begins on page 284 offer a fuller picture, in any given decade, than the one presented here. Yet each of these anthologies only ranged backward a generation or two, so I'm hoping the present compilation will provide more of a panoramic overview. (Two recent anthologies deserve special mention: *Nebraska Presence*, edited by Greg Kosmicki and Mary K. Stillwell, and *A Sandhills Reader*, edited by Mark Sanders.)

And who is a "Nebraska" author? My friend Jeanetta Calhoun Mish defines Oklahoma literature as being made up of writers who identify, or self-identify, "by birth, by raising, by family, by residence, or by choice" with the state, which seemed like a fair approach to take with the present anthology. As I compiled *Nebraska Poetry*, it was not my intention to make this a "greatest hits" collection; rather, I wanted to make the book as broadly inclusive as possible in order to provide, in a single volume, a long view of how Nebraska poetry has evolved over the years. I started out with a core historical list that included Cather, Neihardt, Kees, and Eiseley, expanded it to include the poets of the "second renaissance," then moved backward and forward in time to encompass what I think are some of the state's most representative and enduring poems of the past 150 years. I consulted the existing anthologies and guidebooks, read as many poets' selected poems or individual books of poetry as I had time to work my way through, and ranged widely in the secondary literature. In addition to the "Rushmore" names, I also wanted to include a rich array of younger writers who are redefining what poetry from and about Nebraska might represent. To each of the contemporary poets invited to contribute, in addition to a selection of their own poems, I asked them to recommend two or three of their favorite Nebraska poems—in many cases, the comments they included with their nominations are included as footnotes to the poems included here. Ultimately, the eighty-three poets featured here represent my own personal canon of Nebraska poets, as subjective as that selection must inevitably be.

If Mari Sandoz were alive today, would she still ask, "Where is the writer with the gusto, the wild immeasurable power, the wide horizons, the sense of the universal in man, and his infinite variety?" It might not be possible to find all those traits in a single author, but as a group, I'm confident the poets gathered in the following pages answer her call. In part, my aim here has been to consolidate Nebraska poets' central place—both geographically and historically—within the broader landscape and literary history of the Great Plains and the "wide horizons" of the United States writ large.

And I hope a copy of *Nebraska Poetry* will find its way into school and public libraries, school curricula, writing workshops, bookshelves and bookstores throughout the state. Moreover, I envision the anthology being used for all sorts of teaching and mentoring opportunities; may it inspire young writers and readers to learn about and engage with our state's rich literary heritage while at the same time imagining its many possible futures. What will that landscape look like in 2067, on the occasion of Nebraska's bicentennial? Until then, Sheldon's "great book" continues to be written.

Norman, Oklahoma

Orasmus Charles Dake

(1832–1875)

Born in Portage, New York, Dake became an abolitionist newspaper editor in Illinois in his twenties while accompanying Abraham Lincoln during presidential campaign trips. After being ordained a minister, he and his wife moved to Omaha in 1863 and then to Fremont to build St. James Episcopal church, where he wrote Nebraska Legends and Poems *(1871), the first book published in the newly formed state. He was also appointed the first professor of English literature at the University of Nebraska in 1871, a few years before he died of a cerebral hemorrhage at the age of forty-three.*

Graping*

Down by the dull Cahokia,
Just back from a sandy shore,
You and I went a-graping,
In the pleasant days of yore.
We sat in the glancing shadows,
Or roamed in the open sun;
But of grapes – alas! my darling –
We fetched not a single one.

Our baskets came back empty,
But our hearts were full of dreams,
Inwrought with the warm October
And the sunset's mellow beams.
O sweet through the fading grasses
Wandered the wind's low moan,
And, piping their cheerful signals,
Went birds to a summer zone.

---

* Stephen Behrendt writes, "Dake traces in this gentle but moving poem his family's growth and removal from Illinois to Nebraska, the loss of three children (including two by drowning), and the prospect of growing old, his own children departed for more western homes and his own journey having run its course." Headnote source: Hansen and Dush, *Nebraska Authors*, 2013.

Your hand in my own was resting,
But few were the words we spoke;
And our pitiless companions
Shot at us many a joke.
But little we cared, my darling;
We had plighted our secret truth,
And the world seemed a purple vine-land,
Hung full for the wants of youth.

Then, ere the leaves had fallen,
Or cold blew the northern gale –
Ere the sun swam low in the tropics,
Or the skies were chilly and pale,
The villagers all came trooping –
The greatest as well as the least –
To hear our vow's confession
Before the surpliced priest.

And out through Autumn's glories,
Or ever the day was done,
We had crossed broad river and prairie,
In the track of the hazy sun.
And the still night closed around us,
And Dian smiled bright above
Our shrine of the perfumed Hymen,
And the sacrifice of love.

Oh, swift the years as the passage
Of pigeons with silvery wings;
And deep in their silence is hidden
All tender and holy things –
The smiles, the kisses, the rapture,
The sighs, the unsealing of tears,
The darkness that fills with amazement,
The light in the west that cheers.

They are full of children's voices,
And songs by the cradle sung;
Of the shadowy gleam of faces –
Forever fair and young –

That paled in their opening promise,
And under the willows hide.
Ah, Heaven seems far less distant
Since the little ones have died!

And once again we are graping,
But not near the dear old home;
New lands are ever unstable –
Their people like Arabs roam.
We follow our children westward;
They will follow theirs to the sea.
Few men in the land are settled,
Or know where their graves shall be.

I like, in the mild October,
These rides in the country air,
The plats 'neath the swaying woodlands,
And the sunlight flickering there.
I love the merry laughter
Of the groups at the clustered vine,
And the glimpse of faces rosy
As Moenads flushed with wine.

For, like a wind that freshens
One dropping and moving slow,
These things throw over my spirit
The spell of the long-ago;
And I'm proud that these young people,
Like those of our youthful days,
Have pleasure in simple pleasures,
And love the old-fashioned ways.

But, for us, the scramble is ended,
'Tis time to be sober and still;
We are nearing the mist-covered river –
Are down at the foot of the hill.
Our baskets have ever been empty –
A trifle our slender store;
Yet only for you and the children
Have I ever wished for more.

I hope, when the final summons
Is sped from the ghostly king,
Afar to a peaceful country
Together our souls may wing; –
Together may live in glory,
And round us the children play,
As once in the long-gone summers,
Ere some were taken away.

But now, my arm for the wagon!
The horses are placed abreast,
For the home-bound sun is nearing
His gate in the golden west:
And the wind, with murmur tender,
Dies out in a long, long sigh;
And the bird to his mate is calling
That the chill, dark night is nigh.

Lucy Martin Bullock

(ca. 1855–?)

Bullock was the daughter of C. D. Martin, a missionary and newspaperman who settled in Dakota County, Nebraska Territory, in the 1850s and wrote barely fictionalized accounts about the residents of Dakota City. Bullock joined the Women's Christian Temperance Union, which saw active societies spring up in Nebraska in the 1870s. The national Decoration Day observance, when Americans decorated graves of the Civil War dead with flowers on May 30, began in 1868 and occasioned countless patriotic poems.

Decoration Day

Adown the sunny, dusty street
A little child was trudging on,
One dimpled hand a banner grasped,
The other filled with lilac bloom.

"Why haste thee so, with flag and bloom?
The crowds are coming, little lass,
With banners waving, drums abeat –
Stay here with me and let them pass."

"Oh, no!" she cried, "my flowers may fade,
I *must* be there before they come,
On papa's grave this flag I'll place,
And then I'll wait till they are done."

Oh, soldier's child! Thy tender heart
For father's sake the honor craves,
Assured that others, bearing blooms
Will decorate anew his grave.

Wave, flag of freedom, well thy folds
Were born along to victory's heights
By heroes brave, whose graves today
We decorate 'neath stars and stripes.

For long ago, in spring-time fair
Beneath that flag they marched away,
Undaunted hearts, to fight for right,
They bore their part in freedom's fray.

Oh, Decoration day so fair,
With buds and blossoms for each tomb;
Oh, day of days thy sunshine bright
Bathes every mound, dispels the gloom.

Anew we gather where they lie,
Each soldier's grave is marked the same,
One silent band where rank is naught,
Their names are green in memory's chain.

Edwin Ford Piper

(1871–1939)

Born in Auburn, Nebraska, Piper based much of his poetry on his experience of living among homesteaders and cattlemen in the 1880s. He received BA and MA degrees from the University of Nebraska and taught for the UNL English department for two years before joining the University of Iowa faculty for the remainder of his career. Writing in Poetry *magazine, Harriet Monroe called Piper's* Barbed Wire and Wayfarers *"a broken epic of our heroic period, our pioneer period of adventure in the wide spaces of the West" (Oct. 1924).*

Dry Bones

Springtime outran the furrowings of raw sod;
There must be bread: in August the bonepickers
Go harvesting the prairie, dragging out –
Rich roof for hundred-legs and scurrying beetles –
From the fingers of the grass and spiderweb
Long curving rib and broad white shoulder-blade.
They pay a dollar for a ton in town.

The square, squat houses, the low shedlike stores
Weathering unpainted, toe the littered street
That finds the railway station. By the track,
A fenced lot heaped with bleaching skeletons, –
Mountainous wreckage, shin and back confused,
Crowned with horned skulls grotesquely menacing.

So ends the buffalo. Five years since he tossed
In great earth-shaking herds his shaggy mane;
Now not one calf. Once furious bulls did roar
The challenge moving terribly to fight.

Dry bones – the price one dollar for a ton.

Big Swimming*

Rain on the high prairies,
In dusk of autumnal hills;
Under the creaking saddle
My cheerless pony plods. . . .

Down where the obscure water
Lapping the lithe willows
Sunders the chilling plain –
Rusty-hearted and travel-worn –
We set our bodies
To the November flood.

The farther shore is a cloud
Beyond midnight. . . .

Big swimming.

Indian Counsel

Do not be always looking on the fire –
It will dry up your eyes and make you blind.

Look upon falling snow and running water,
On crinkleroot and brightening willow bark;
The dancing crane, the coyote, and the moon;
On laughing children.

No, not on the fire –
You will go blind.

---

* In his prefatory note to *Paintrock Road* (1927), Piper notes that " 'Big Swimming' is a name for uncrossable water."

You Too

You too
Break over the gap
Between highest emotion
And trivial doing.

You too,
After the sunset,
Shall be broken in pieces
In a windowless room.

In Dust and Gilt

Epitaph – died of bibliography.

Hartley Burr Alexander

(1873–1939)

Born in Lincoln, Alexander grew up in Syracuse, Nebraska, then attended the University of Nebraska in the 1890s, where he was an influential member of a dynamic literary coterie that included Willa Cather and Louise Pound. After receiving his PhD from Columbia, Alexander returned to UNL, where he taught philosophy for two decades (1908–28) and cultivated an interest in metaphysics, mythology, and Indian art and philosophy. Best remembered now for his inscriptions on the state capitol, Joslyn Art Museum, Rockefeller Center, and elsewhere, his poems articulate a mythic vision of culture on the prairies. Here, Alexander assumes that readers will immediately compare his poem to Whitman's "Pioneers! O Pioneers!" and to Cather's 1913 novel, O Pioneers!

Pioneers!

Pioneers, O Pioneers!
Bring the wagon, yoke the steers,
Cast behind all doubts and fears!
Forward, through the waiting years!
Pioneers, O Pioneers!

'Tis your toil shall break the road;
'Tis your backs shall bear the load;
'Tis your souls must feel the goad!

Where ye sow shall others reap;
Others laugh where ye must weep;
But your deathless souls shall keep
Vigil through the waiting years,
Pioneers, O Pioneers!

Snap! Crack!

Thud and thwack!
'Tis the chanty of the plains

Never, never, turn we back!
O'er the trails that rise and dip,
To the whistling of the whip
And the clanking of the chains

Snap! Crack!

Thud and thwack!
Sing the chanty of the Plains

Never, never, turn we back!

Willa Cather

(1873–1947)

Although best known for her novels, short stories, and essays, Willa Cather's first published book, April Twilights *(1903), was a collection of poems. She began publishing verse while a student at the University of Nebraska, but the poems of* April Twilights *date from her years in Pittsburgh. Bernice Slote notes that Cather "was not ready to love Nebraska in her poems," that "April enchantments were tenuous and bittersweet" since she associated spring with the old world, not the new. Yet "with a certain distance of time and experience," writes Slote – notably, by the time she published* O Pioneers! *in 1913 – Cather "turned about and found Arcadia in her own West," even though that Arcadia had by then mostly vanished.*

Prairie Dawn

A crimson fire that vanquishes the stars;
A pungent odor from the dusty sage;
A sudden stirring of the huddled herds;
A breaking of the distant table-lands
Through purple mists ascending, and the flare
Of water ditches silver in the light;
A swift, bright lance hurled low across the world;
A sudden sickness for the hills of home.

Prairie Spring

Evening and the flat land,
Rich and somber and always silent;
The miles of fresh-plowed soil,
Heavy and black, full of strength and harshness;
The growing wheat, the growing weeds,
The toiling horses, the tired men;
The long, empty roads,
Sullen fires of sunset, fading,
The eternal, unresponsive sky.
Against all this, Youth,
Flaming like the wild roses,

Singing like the larks over the plowed fields,
Flashing like a star out of the twilight;
Youth with its insupportable sweetness,
Its fierce necessity,
Its sharp desire;
Singing and singing,
Out of the lips of silence,
Out of the earthy dusk.

Margaret Haughawout

(1874–1964)

Haughawout, a contemporary of Willa Cather and Hartley Burr Alexander, was born in Fairmont, Nebraska, earned a BA at Hastings College, and received an MA in English from the University of Nebraska (1903). As a professor of English, Haughawout taught at Hastings College, Alma College (Michigan), and Kansas State Teachers College and also served as superintendent of schools in Fillmore County, Nebraska. Although beloved by her students, during the Depression she lost her job at the Teachers College after "rankling the administration," according to Randy Roberts: "She had her students read contemporary modernist literature while the rest of the faculty stayed in the nineteenth century. Her insistence that James Joyce and D. H. Lawrence were worthy of study shocked some students" (Lost Writers of the Plains). *Her only published verse collection,* Sheep's Clothing, *appeared in 1929.*

Foiled

I'd like to say that word again . . . for three
There were that took effect . . . and one that failed
No time to cause your harried tragic face
When I returned . . . But if I said that worst
One to you now . . . I might . . . But you would still
Be plucking out a blade of grass, hunting
For four-leaved clovers, slowly plaiting edge
Of handkerchief, white dreams in your dark eyes,
And I should know futility. You are
So slim I could unjoint your bones. And yet
You have escaped me! In what deep pool then
I cannot fathom have you found content?

Ruthless

And if it caused me pain, why, there was pain.
If I grubbed out some roots, those spared could grow.
And if I pruned out perfect blooming sprays,
Those kept had air and space, the rest might go.

However tall and fair, the ship that's moored
   Will never bring home rich brocades and tea;
But if it someday reaches Samarcand,
   Must wrench its anchors and put out to sea.

To a Good Girl

Like some chaste maenad whom the storm cannot seduce
   You sweep into my frugal room.
Relentless steel is in your powerful stride; bright, loose
   Spun gold, wind-swept, your hair. No doom

Can quite confuse your insolent young strength; the hue
   Of softest rose upon your damask cheek
Belies no whit the pitiless and level blue
   With which you meet my gaze. You reek

Of goodness, definite and hard; efficiency;
   Determined, fixed, and sealed you know
The pale of right; and wrong you know you'll never know. I see
   You nail your colors to the mast! You throw

Away your scabbard! Wrong but stirs your glorious young wrath!
I pray no weak nor inefficient thing may cross your glowing path!

At a Teachers College

What flamed across your path at this late day, burned out,
   And left you looking tired?
The years you should have spent here, held you festive rout,
   Then red-cheeked and admired?
Or by something sacrificial, immolating, was your soul
   In self-denial fired?
. . . Or shiftless, dreamless, year by year, a wit of clay,
   Have you been slowly mired?

A Learned Lady

"Had I your eyes," pert girls have said,
   "I'd use them." And they would.
For men have never tempted me.
   They said, "She's good. She's good."

I envied those who danced and kissed.
   And even those who fell.
They learned, I knew, things I had missed.
   While I earned my D.L.L.

I planned to burn one candle up,
   To fling one merry dance.
I did. And every male I've met
   Has given me a chance.

Enclosed in gilt parenthesis
   Are words of double glow.
Have scales dropped from my eyes, think you?
   Or do they know I know?

John G. Neihardt
(1881–1973)

If Nebraska had a Mount Rushmore of poets, Neihardt would be our Jefferson – and perhaps our Roosevelt too. Born in Illinois, Neihardt lived in a sod house in Kansas before moving to Wayne, Nebraska, with his mother and sisters at the age of ten. Moving to Bancroft at the turn of the century, he began publishing his earliest work: short stories, a narrative poem called The Divine Enchantment *(1900), and the lyric collection* A Bundle of Myrrh *(1907). He was named Poet Laureate of Nebraska in 1921 and went on to teach at the University of Missouri for many years. He is best known for* Black Elk Speaks *(1932) and* A Cycle of the West *(1949); the latter was selected by the Millennium Committee in the year 2000 as "one of the world's 2000 most important books of all time from Homer to Hemingway."*

If This Be Sin

Can this be sin?
This ecstasy of arms and eyes and lips,
This thrilling of caressing finger-tips,
This toying with incomparable hair?
(I close my dazzled eyes, you are so fair!)
This answer of caress to fond caress,
This exquisite maternal tenderness?
How could so much of beauty enter in,
If this be sin?

Can it be wrong?
This cry of flesh to flesh, so like a song?
This fusing of two atoms with a kiss,
Hurled to the black and pitiless abyss?

Can it be crime
That we should snatch one happy hour from Time –
Time that has naught but death for you and me?
(How soon, O Dearest, shall we cease to be!)
And could one frenzied hour of love or lust
Augment the final tragedy of dust?

Although we be two sinners burned with bliss,
Kiss me again, that warm round woman's kiss!
Close up the gates of gold! I go not in –
If this be sin.

Easter

Once more the northbound Wonder
Brings back the goose and crane,
Prophetic Sons of Thunder,
Apostles of the Rain.

In many a battling river
The broken gorges boom;
Behold, the Mighty Giver
Emerges from the tomb!

Now robins chant the story
Of how the wintry sward
Is litten with the glory
Of the Angel of the Lord.

His countenance is lightning
And still His robe is snow,
As when the dawn was brightening
Two thousand years ago.

O who can be a stranger
To what has come to pass?
The Pity of the Manger
Is mighty in the grass!

Undaunted by Decembers,
The sap is faithful yet.
The giving Earth remembers,
And only men forget.

from The Death of Crazy Horse

In this selection from The Song of the Indian Wars *(1925), from his epic five-part* A Cycle of the West, *Neihardt focuses on the last days of the famed Oglala Lakota warrior in northwestern Nebraska in 1877, who surrendered to US troops and was fatally wounded by a military guard while allegedly resisting imprisonment. The following excerpt – from the second half of the poem – takes up the story when Crazy Horse is arrested at the Spotted Tail Agency and transferred to Camp Robinson.*

They found him in the camp of Spotted Tail,
A lonely figure with a face of care.
"I am afraid of what might happen there"
He said. "So many listen what I say
And look and look. I will not run away
I want my people here. You have my guns."

But half a world away the mighty ones
Had spoken words like bullets in the dark
That wreak the rage of blindness on a mark
They can not know.

Then spoke the one who led
The soldiers: "Not a hair upon your head
Shall suffer any harm if you will go
To Robinson for just a day or so
And have a parley with the soldier chief."
He spoke believing and he won belief,
So Crazy Horse went riding down the west;
And neither he nor any trooper guessed
What doom now made a rutted wagon road
The highway to a happier abode
Where all the dead are splendidly alive
And summer lingers and the bison thrive
Forever.

If the better hope be true,
There was a gate of glory yawning through
The sunset when the little cavalcade
Approached the fort.

The populous parade,
The straining hush that somehow wasn't peace,
The bristling troops, the Indian police
Drawn up as for a battle! What was wrong?
What made them hustle Crazy Horse along
Among the gleaming bayonets and eyes?
There swept a look of quizzical surprise
Across his face. He struggled with the guard.
Their grips were steel; their eyes were cold and hard –
Like bayonets.

There was a door flung wide.
The soldier chief would talk with him inside
And all be well at last!

The stifling, dim
Interior poured terror over him.
He blinked about – and saw the iron bars.
O nevermore to neighbor with the stars
Or know the simple goodness of the sun!
Did some swift vision of a doom begun
Reveal the monstrous purpose of a lie –
The desert island and the alien sky,
The long and lonely ebbing of a life?

The glimmer of a whipped-out butcher knife
Dismayed the shrinking squad, and once again
Men saw a face that many better men
Had died to see! Brown arms that once were kind,
A comrade's arms, whipped round him from behind,
Went crimson with a gash and dropped aside.
"Don't touch me! I am Crazy Horse!" he cried,
And, leaping doorward, charged upon the world
To meet the end. A frightened soldier hurled
His weight behind a jabbing belly-thrust,
And Crazy Horse plunged headlong in the dust,
A writhing heap. The momentary din
Of struggle ceased. The people, closing in,
Went ominously silent for a space,
And one could hear men breathing round the place

Where lay the mighty. Now he strove to rise,
The wide blind stare of anguish in his eyes,
And someone shouted "*Kill that devil quick!*"

A throaty murmur and a running click
Of gun-locks woke among the crowding Sioux,
And many a soldier whitened. Well they knew
What pent-up hate the moment might release
To drop upon the bungled farce of peace
A bloody curtain.

One began to talk;
His tongue was drunken and his face was chalk;
But when a halfbreed shouted what he spoke
The crowd believed, so few had seen the stroke,
Nor was there any bleeding of the wound.
It seemed the chief had fallen sick and swooned;
Perhaps a little rest would make him strong!
And silently they watched him borne along,
A sagging bundle, dear and mighty yet,
Though from the sharp face, beaded with the sweat
Of agony, already peered the ghost.

They laid him in an office of the post,
And soldiers, forming in a hollow square,
Held back the people. Silence deepened there.
A little while it seemed the man was dead,
He lay so still. The west no longer bled;
Among the crowd the dusk began to creep.
Then suddenly, as startled out of sleep
By some old dream-remembered night alarm,
He strove to shout, half rose upon an arm
And glared about him in the lamp-lit place.

The flare across the ashes of his face
Went out. He spoke; and, leaning where he lay,
Men strained to gather what he strove to say,
So hard the panting labor of his words.
"I had my village and my pony herds
On Powder where the land was all my own.

I only wanted to be let alone.
I did not want to fight. The Gray Fox sent
His soldiers. We were poorer when they went;
Our babies died, for many lodges burned
And it was cold. We hoped again and turned
Our faces westward. It was just the same
Out yonder on the Rosebud. Gray Fox came.
The dust his soldiers made was high and long.
I fought him and I whipped him. Was it wrong
To drive him back? That country was my own.
I only wanted to be let alone.
I did not want to see my people die.
They say I murdered Long Hair and they lie.
His soldiers came to kill us and they died."

He choked and shivered, staring hungry-eyed
As though to make the most of little light.
Then like a child that feels the clutching night
And cries the wilder, deeming it in vain,
He raised a voice made lyrical with pain
And terror of a thing about to be.
"*I want to see you. Father! Come to me!*
I want to see you. Mother!" O'er and o'er
His cry assailed the darkness at the door;
And from the gloom beyond the hollow square
Of soldiers, quavered voices of despair:
"*We can not come! They will not let us come!*"

But when at length the lyric voice was dumb
And Crazy Horse was nothing but a name,
There was a little withered woman came
Behind a bent old man. Their eyes were dim.
They sat beside the boy and fondled him,
Remembering the little names he knew
Before the great dream took him and he grew
To be so mighty. And the woman pressed
A hand that men had feared against her breast
And swayed and sang a little sleepy song.

Out yonder in the village all night long
There was a sound of mourning in the dark.
And when the morning heard the meadowlark,
The last great Sioux rode silently away.
Before the pony-drag on which he lay
An old man tottered. Bowed above the bier,
A little wrinkled woman kept the rear
With not a sound and nothing in her eyes.

Who knows the crumbling summit where he lies
Alone among the Badlands? Kiotes prowl
About it, and the voices of the owl
Assume the day-long sorrow of the crows,
These many grasses and these many snows.

Ione Gardner

(1900–?)

Gardner, born in Omaha, attended UNL in the 1920s, where she helped edit the student publication Awgwan. *Six of her poems appear in* Nebraska Verse, 1923–1924, *a collection chosen by Christopher Morley, John G. Neihardt, and Percy MacKaye from a shortlist recommended by Louise Pound, Constance Syford, Hartley Burr Alexander, Sherlock B. Gass, and J. A. Rice Jr. After marrying Laurence Noyes in 1927, the couple moved to his hometown of Waterloo, Iowa, then to Elkhorn, Nebraska, where she apparently "put away all things" related to poetry. "Tall Girl" was reprinted in Humphreys's* Poems by Nebraska Poets *(1941).*

I Have Put Away All Things

I have put away all things that spoke of you.
In my house there is no book, no chair, no song
For you to hide in. I have raised dark blinds
To shut out the moon – the moon and the meadows
Steeped in dew.

Just when I thought that I was free
The wind came – calling your name.
And when I fled to the safety of the streets
A beggar-boy with eyes like yours
Smiled at me.

Tall Girl

Tall Girl in a red gown
Swinging down a dull street
On a gray morning.

Tall Girl, wearing a raglan coat
Over the red dress that touches your ankles;
With bobbed yellow hair,
Streaked with brown
Where the wet brush has smoothed it.

Your eyes are cool
As shadowless pools,
Your chin is scornful,
Your lips firm,
Your shoulders hold off
The world.

Tall Girl, all women
Wore that air of triumph
Once.

Clarissa Bucklin

(1904–1980)

A writer, editor, and painter, after graduating from the University of Nebraska, Bucklin edited Nebraska Art and Artists *(1932), the first comprehensive book of early Nebraska artistic activity from the pre-territorial period through statehood and into the early 1930s. She was a member of The Quill society of women writers and the Lincoln Artists' Guild and published poems in* The Crisis *and* Prairie Schooner. *Her poems "Inhibitions" (1928) and "Midwest Minerva" (1939), in which the Catherian speaker of the latter poem longs for "old Greece and old Cathay" amidst "Midwest false-front architecture," appear in Humphreys's* Poems by Nebraska Poets *(1940).*

Inhibitions

I want to snatch the corner of my blue shirt
And hold it out against the wind and dance;
But my father was a Puritan,
And his father's father's father,
And – the world might look askance!

I want to make a song of love and passion
And sing it loud beneath an echoing sky;
But my mother was a Puritan,
And her mother's mother's mother.
And – how the world might cry!

I want to talk to wicked men and women;
Have someone think my mouth is fire to kiss;
But my father and my mother,
And my mother's father's mother,
And my father's mother's father,
Were Puritan, you see,
And – What a lot I miss!

Midwest Minerva

Though "raised" with Midwest false-front architecture
She dreamed of old cathedrals, like a fool,
And symphonies were matters for conjecture
While playing organ at the Sunday School.

She longed for poetry and contemplation,
The quietness of pines and paper birch;
But cousins, nieces, all of her "relation"
Brought picnic lunch and babies after church.

At Ladies' Aid she hid her faint dejection
And smiled and sewed and listened while they told
How foreigners and heathens lack perfection,
Praised all the new and censured all the old.

Her hands were kind in sickness, quick at quilting,
Neighborly her acts and full her day;
She did her housework to an inner lilting,
While visioning old Greece and old Cathay.

They praised her pickles and her jelly-making,
But said her nose was always in a book.
What use, they mused, such excellence in baking,
When men think brains are wasted on a cook?

She copied verse she wanted to remember,
And did not seem to hear, much less resent,
The phrase folks thought should burn her like an ember –
That she was born "Old Maid" and "different."

Helene Magaret

(1906–1998)

Born in Omaha, a contemporary (and friend) of Loren Eiseley, Magaret worked as a foreign correspondent and translator in Spain in the 1920s, served as Chilean Nobel laureate Gabriela Mistral's interpreter in New York City during the early years of the Depression, and went on to receive an MA and PhD from the Iowa Writers' Workshop. Most active as a poet in the 1930s, she served as chair of the English department at Marymount College in Tarrytown, New York, before retiring to Omaha. The following poems appear in her collection Change of Season *(1941).*

Song of the Answerer
(A reply to Walt Whitman)

I

I celebrate America,
For every atom belonging to America belongs to you and me,
And is a part of us.
Walt Whitman, come down!
And I will sing your message back to you.
Now, in the fourth month, shoulder to shoulder let us talk.

I celebrate the shanties of river-rats no less than the skyscrapers eighty stories high,
The widow reading, "We regret we must waive dividends again,"
The Chairman of the Board still drawing his hundred thousand twice a year.
I am satisfied with what I see:
Sharecroppers starving in the South, mobs milling in Detroit,
The machine guns down the alleys of Chicago,
Thieves, murderers, men who traffic in women,
I give all the same, I receive all the same.
"And there will never be any more perfection than there is now."

II

I celebrate America,
And beyond America I celebrate the world.

The new-born babe in its mother's lap, the father knee-deep in African swamps,
The dead in the gutters of Teruel, and bodies floating down the Hwang-Ho River.
"Clear and sweet is my soul, and clear and sweet is all that is not my soul."

Because we have no God in America,
Does anyone think it is wrong for the Germans to have a God,
Who commands his people, and feeds his sheep, and drives the money-changers out?
Does anyone complain that in Russia Trotsky had to flee,
And Gorki was murdered, and the poets sold their souls to breathe a little longer?
"It is well – against such I say not a word."

All good things are waiting.
I say the deep trenches are being dug for the happiness of men.
The gas masks being given free, the big ships growing bigger.
I say we should thank Heaven for liquid fire, for submarines and airplanes.
And for the new bombs that can destroy a city fifty miles away.
"Has anyone supposed it lucky to be born?
I hasten to inform him or her it is just as lucky to die."

Prairie Women

Stolid the prairie women are,
With rugged hands and backs that bow
In unremitting servitude
Above the churn and plow.

Men ever turn to lighter loves
With slender breasts and unbound hair,
And ever follow where the winds
Are gentler and more fair.

While prairie women home at night,
Weary of treading fields forlorn,
Stare in their mirrors long, and hate
The tyranny of corn.

In Answer to a Letter (III)

If you are disappointed, I am sorry.
Then I must counsel you to cut the stone
Of some untouched and more resistant quarry,
Where heart is intellect and flesh is bone.
As woman, I cannot be satisfied
To rest upon the word; and passionate,
I cannot put my other needs aside
Even now, when the hour for love is late.
But could we crush these mountains into dust,
These separating prairies, you would learn
How every philosophic theory must
Increase in power when two undisguised
Lovers acknowledge it, how truth will burn
More brightly as the flesh is recognized.

Come Out of the Cold

Come out of the cold, and out of misery.
Climb where these rocks above wet samphire tower
Like women waiting for the fishboats. We
Discover here one famine-stricken flower.
This is the end of loneliness, this space
Torn from the roaring chaos where we are . . .
This moment when I look upon your face
And find it constant as the northern star.
Here with its roots in granite one bright clover
Struggles for strength to feed three butterflies.
On this gaunt cliff that only terns flyer over . . .
Listen, Beloved, hear the winds arise!
There is a wind called War, and its black flame
Withers the world. There is a wind called Hunger,
And there are bitter winds that have no name
Save Death. All night they blow! When we were younger
We never walked with winter on the bluff,
We never ran between land's edge and sea.
Here on this rocky ledge give all to love.
Come out of the cold, and out of misery.

Loren Eiseley

(1907–1977)

Although born in the city of Lincoln, Nebraska, from the earliest days of his boyhood Loren Eiseley was drawn to the "rougher margins" of the Great Plains – in the preface to The Innocent Assassins *(1973), he presents his work as "the poems of a bone hunter and a naturalist." A "modern Thoreau" with a millennial outlook, Eiseley studied poetry and anthropology at the University of Nebraska, contributed to the Federal Writers' Project* Guide to the Cornhusker State *(1939), and went on to become one of the great writer-scientists of the twentieth century.*

Now the Singing Is Done

They are burning the cornfields now. In the mellow dusk,
In the leaf-mold moon when the pumpkins go to town,
They are burning the cornfields up, and the wind-warped smoke
Trails mountain-blue in the fields and the stubborn brown

Hills go quietly dark. Now the singing is done
In the harvesters' throats. As the dense grass catches fire,
I think of the fuel I have been to a fiercer flame –
In the darkness I shrink and yet with the old desire

Tormented I stand but know in my veins no more
The rush of the blood. On that mad invisible tide
I have leaned the last time. The iron and flint at the core
Strike darkness at last. I am glad that the night is wide.

I am glad that over my shoulder no greater shadow than this
Leans . . . you are gone. The world is as still as death.
I have had it all – the bitter loving by stealth
And the open love. For the harsh and the tortured breath

I give my thanks – for the bodies I could not hold,
For the mouths abandoned and lost. Far better be sieve to the deep
Waters that always move than to dry to an acrid pool,
Be a mocker at love . . . *I shall sleep with fire when I sleep.*

The High Plains

I found the pink catlinite bowl of an Indian pipe
and an iron arrowhead
once in the middle of a road in Kansas.
I suppose the road graders had cut through a house pit,
but this is the way
one culture tumbles into another.

In the dust-bowl days
when the soil was mostly
traveling
by air
you could find lying mixed on the hardpan
antique barbed wire,
a branding iron from Texas,
a fragment of
whiskey jug,
mammoth teeth,
and flint knives.
The debris covered ten thousand years and it wasn't much,
considering the time,
nor was it easy
to measure the intervals
from one chipped stone
to another.
They had all sifted down from their previous levels as the wind blew
the earth away
and on the hardpan
they huddled together,
the artifacts of the literate
and the illiterate,
not too dissimilar
in final purpose.
Looking on there one saw everything, including one's self, in final perspective.
Five hundred human generations
leave very little.
On the high plains
the soft stuff goes first
and that includes
man.

The Condor*

The great bird moves its feathers on the air
like fingers playing on an instrument,
the instrument of wind; it climbs and scarcely moves
                                        while steady thermals push
                                        its giant wings still higher till it soars
beyond my sight completely, though it peers
                    through strange red eyes
                    upon my face below.
Its kind is dying from the earth; its wings
                    create a foolish envy among men.
Its shadow knew the mammoth and he passed,
                    floated above the sabertooth, now gone,
                    saw the first spearmen on the bison's track,
                    banked sharply, went its way alone.
Its eyes are larger than its searching brain;
                    the creature sees like a satellite,
                    but exists within
                    an ice-age world now dead. This bird cannot
                    understand rifles, multiply its eggs,
                    one hidden on a cliff face all it has.
Its shadow is now passing from the earth
                    just as the mammoth's shadow at high noon.
Something has gone with each of them, the sky
                    is out of balance with the tipping poles.
                    No huge, tusked beast is marching with the ice,
no aerial shadow tracks the passing years.
                    Only below the haze grows deeper still,
                    only the buildings edge up through the murk.
Planes fly, and sometimes crash, but no black wing will write
                    the end of man, as man's end should be written
                    by all the condor wings beneath high heaven.

---

* Jim Cihlar writes, "What other poet could effectively use a line like 'the creature sees like a satellite' or note, scientifically in lines of verse, that the bird's eyes are larger than its brain? Urgent when first published in 1973, this poem's screed against animal and habitat extinction is even more vivid and necessary today."

We Are the Scriveners

I have not seen her in forty years.
She is old now or lies in one of those midwestern farm cemeteries where
no one remembers for long, because everyone
leaves for the cities. She was young, with freckles
and a wide generous mouth, a good girl to have
loved for a lifetime but the world
always chooses otherwise, or we ourselves
in blindness. I would not remember so clearly save that here
by a prairie slough sprinkled with the leaves of autumn
the drying mud on the shore shows the imprint
of southbound birds. I am too old to travel,
but I suddenly realize how a man in Sumer
                                        half the world and millennia away
saw the same imprint and thought
                            there is a way of saying upon clay, fire-hardened,
                            there is a way of saying
                            "loneliness"
                            a way of saying
                            "where are you?" across the centuries
                            a way of saying
                            "forgive me"
                            a way of saying
              "We were young. I remember, and this, this clay
                            imprinted with the feet of birds
                            will reach you somewhere
                            somehow
                            if it takes eternity to answer."
There were men like this in Sumer, or who wept among the
                                                        autumn papyrus leaves in Egypt.
                                                        We are the scriveners who with pain
                                                                                outlasted our bodies.

Lavon Jarvis

(1910–?)

While living in Grand Island, Nebraska, Jarvis served as executive secretary for the Nebraska League of Women Voters before moving to Fresno, California, and serving in the Women's Army Auxiliary Corps during World War II. "No Cathedral" and "Spring Returns to the Prairie" were featured in Henry Harrison's Minnesota and Nebraska Poets *anthology in 1937;* Prairie Schooner *published a drastically abridged version of the latter poem in its Spring 1939 issue, which featured a note by Weldon Kees on Depression-era little magazines.*

No Cathedral

No cathedral has our prairie.
Religion
Is a practical thing of
Square stone edifices with
Roomy auditoriums for Y.M.C.A. speakers or the
Girl evangelist from Dubuque;
And basement kitchens
Serving weekly creamed-chicken-on-biscuit suppers.
No cathedrals unless they be
Its cylindrical silos and grain elevators
Haloed by the pink inviolability of setting suns,
Or railroad stations resplendent in Gothic
Windows and delicately veined pillars shipped
From marble quarries in Vermont.
No candelabraed shrine. No imposing organ
Weeping invocations through drafty
Vaults of ancient limestone ornately
Byzantine and buttressed.
. . . Only the clattered hymns of
Threshing machines and reapers –
And the booming basso of train
Callers: Cedar Rapids, Omaha
And all points west.

Spring Returns to the Prairie

Farmers are losing their winter lethargy,
Brief the hours, now, of fingered seed catalogues.
The earth is stirring, warmth is
Beginning to spread over it like
A sweet benediction, a fertile promise . . .
Storm fences stacked in the pastures; round,
Rusty bundles done with their season's lonely vigil . . .
The pungent smell of burning tumbleweeds raked into neat hills,
Licked by greedy tongues of flame – offering to Ostara; of snow
Melted on manure piles . . .
Polishing of plows in barnyards, mending of harnesses . . .
Talk of seed corn over the milking, the watering
Tanks – hatcheries and Plymouth Rocks and Buff Orpingtons . . .
A fuzz of green creeping across the fields,
Buds swelling on the wild plum thickets, flecking the willow saplings
Growing along the creek like a fringe of rushes . . .

No second spring? Perhaps not to novelists, to hypochondriacs
And motion picture barons, but each year it keeps its
Tryst with the prairie, down where the river
Begins to melt blue, where the johnny-jump-ups prick the patient sod
With tender green blades and truant youngsters dig for fish worms –
As inevitable as the white ache of Easter lilies –
Deep in the consciousness of farmers all through the barrenness of
Winter fields corn stubbled and desolate with brittleness . . .
Dreamed of, planned for – the north section in
Rye this year, the south in potatoes . . .

Tillie Olsen

(1912–2007)

Born in Omaha to a family of Jewish Socialists from Russia, Tillie (Lerner) Olsen dropped out of Central High School and was jailed in Kansas City while organizing packinghouse workers. A longtime member of the Communist Party USA, Olsen championed labor, social, and political causes throughout her life. "I Want You Women up North to Know," written in San Francisco when she was twenty-two, originally appeared in The Partisan *in 1934, a magazine published by the John Reed Club. Olsen won support for her writing in the mid-1930s but put aside writing until the publication of the highly regarded collection of stories* Tell Me a Riddle *in 1961. Olsen's novel,* Yonnondio *(1974), is set in a meatpacking city based on Omaha, and her nonfiction work* Silences *(1974) explores the reasons that often deterred women from becoming writers.*

I Want You Women up North to Know

Based on a Letter by Felipe Ibarro
in New Masses, *January 9th, 1934*

I want you women up north to know
how those dainty children's dresses you buy
    at macy's, wannamakers, gimbels, marshall fields,
are dyed in blood, are stitched in wasting flesh,
down in San Antonio, "where sunshine spends the winter."

I want you women up north to see
the obsequious smile, the salesladies trill
    "exquisite work, madame, exquisite pleats"
vanish into a bloated face, ordering more dresses,
    gouging the wages down,
dissolve into maria, ambrosa, catalina,
    stitching these dresses from dawn to night,
    In blood, in wasting flesh.

Catalina Rodriguez, 24,
    body shrivelled to a child's at twelve,
catalina rodriguez, last stages of consumption,
    works for three dollars a week from dawn to midnight.
A fog of pain thickens over her skull, the parching heat
    breaks over her body,
and the bright red blood embroiders the floor of her room.

White rain stitching the night, the bourgeois poet would say.
white gulls of hands, darting, veering,
white lightning, threading the clouds,
this is the exquisite dance of her hands over the cloth,
and her cough, gay, quick, staccato,
like skeleton's bones clattering,
is appropriate accompaniment for the esthetic dance of her fingers,
and the tremolo, tremolo when the hands tremble with pain.
Three dollars a week,
two fifty-five,
seventy cents a week,
no wonder two thousand eight hundred ladies of joy
are spending the winter with the sun after he goes down –
for five cents (who said this was a rich man's world?) you can
get all the lovin you want
"clap and syph aint much worse than sore fingers, blind eyes, and t.b."

Maria Vasquez, spinster,
for fifteen cents a dozen stitches garments for children
she has never had,
Catalina Torres, mother of four,
to keep the starved body starving, embroiders from dawn to night.
Mother of four, what does she think of,
as the needle pocked fingers shift over the silk –
of the stubble-coarse rags that stretch on her own brood,
and jut with the bony ridge that marks hunger's landscape
of fat little prairie-roll bodies that will bulge in the
silk she needles?
(Be not envious, Catalina Torres, look!
on your own children's clothing, embroidery,
more intricate than any a thousand hands could fashion,
there where the cloth is ravelled, or darned,
designs, multitudinous, complex and handmade by Poverty herself.)
Ambrosa Espinoza trusts in god,
"Todos es de dios, everything is from god,"
through the dwindling night, the waxing day, she bolsters
herself up with it –
but the pennies to keep god incarnate, from ambrosa,
and the pennies to keep the priest in wine,
from ambrosa, ambrosa clothes god and priest with hand-made children's dresses.

Her brother lies on an iron cot, all day and watches,
on a mattress of rags he lies.
For twenty-five years he worked for the railroad, then they laid him off.
    (racked days, searching for work; rebuffs; suspicious eyes of policemen.
    goodbye ambrosa, mebbe in dallas I find work; desperate swing for a
        freight,
    surprised hands, clutching air, and the wheel goes over a leg,
    the railroad cuts it off, as it cut off twenty-five years of his life.)
She says that he prays and dreams of another world, as he lies there, a heaven
    (which he does not know was brought to earth in 1917 in Russia,
    by workers like him).

Women up north, I want you to know
when you finger the exquisite hand-made dresses
what it means, this working from dawn to midnight,
on what strange feet the feverish dawn must come
    to maria, catalina, ambrosa,
how the malignant fingers twitching over the pallid faces jerk them to work,
and the sun and the fever mount with the day –
    long plodding hours, the eyes burn like coals, heat jellies
    the flying fingers,
down comes the night like blindness.
    long hours more with the dim eye of the lamp, the breaking back,
    weariness crawls in the flesh like worms, gigantic like earth's in winter.
And for Catalina Rodriguez comes the night sweat and the blood
    embroidering the darkness.
    for Catalina Torres the pinched faces of four huddled children,
    the naked bodies of four bony children,
    the chant of their chorale of hunger.
And for twenty eight hundred ladies of joy the grotesque act gone over –
    the wink – the grimace – the "feeling like it baby?"
And for Maria Vasquez, spinster, emptiness, emptiness,
    flaming with dresses for children she can never fondle.
And for Ambrosa Espinoza – the skeleton body of her brother on
his mattress of rags, boring twin holes in the dark with his eyes
to the image of christ, remembering a leg, and twenty-five years
cut off from his life by the railroad.

Women up north, I want you to know,
I tell you this can't last forever.

I swear it won't.

Karl Shapiro

(1913–2000)

Born in Baltimore, Shapiro won a Pulitzer Prize and was named Consultant in Poetry to the Library of Congress in 1946, all before the age of thirty-five. His Nebraska connection dates from the years 1956–66, when he edited Prairie Schooner *and taught for the English Department at the University of Nebraska. Stanley Kunitz calls* The Bourgeois Poet *(1964)—the source of "Nebraska" (below)—"simultaneously a book of self-revelation, a poet's zigzag manifesto, and a cry of the heart against the ills of an age." "Western Town" first appeared in* Selected Poems *(1968).*

[Nebraska]

I love Nowhere where the factories die of malnutrition.
I love Nowhere where there are no roads, no rivers, no interesting Indians,
Where history is invented in the History Department and there are no centennials of anything,
Where every tree is planted by hand and has a private tutor,
Where the "parts" have to be ordered and the sky settles all questions,
Where travelers from California bitch at the backwardness and New Yorkers step on the gas in a panic,
Where the grass in winter is gray not brown,
Where the population diminishes.
Here on the boundary of the hired West, equidistant from every tourist office, and the air is washed by distance, here at last there is nothing to recommend.
May no one ever attempt a recommendation; Chicago be as far as Karachi.
Though the warriors come with rockets, may they fall off the trucks.
May the voting be light and the clouds like a cruise and the criminal boredom enter the district of hogs.
I love Nowhere where the human brag is a brag of neither time nor place,
But an elephant house of Smithsonian bones and the white cathedrals of grain,
The feeding-lots in the snow with the steers huddled in symmetrical misery, backs to the sleet,
To beef us up in the Beef State plains, something to look at.

Western Town

Strange western town at the round edge of night,
Into your sleep the broad-shouldered train
Gentles its way, absorbed in its thunderous quiet,
Shearing off porches of carpenter's gothic,
Gathering bulbs and crocuses of electricity.
Now the green blinds of country stores go down
And arches of gold lettering gleam
Like old asbestos in dead movie houses.

Heart-heavy in the cool compartments
The traveling men turn over in their sleep
As the pale squares of light, newspaper thin,
Fall on their eyelids again and again and again,
Plunging the sleepers into a deeper sleep,
A deeper drift of linen than their dream.

Perhaps a single figure is let down
In the hometown dark, or maybe not;
Perhaps only the sleepy sacks of mail
Or a lone coffin come by rail
At rest now, on a sketchy cart. Tomorrow,
Somewhere the city will take the train apart.

Bernice Slote

(1913–1983)

Born in Hickman, Nebraska, Slote received a BA from Nebraska Wesleyan and an MA from the University of Nebraska, where she joined the faculty of the English Department in 1946. Best known as a poetry critic, anthologist, and Cather scholar, she was also an accomplished poet. "Grandfather" first appeared in Prairie Schooner *(Summer 1947), which she went on to edit from 1963 to 1980. In an issue of the journal published in her honor, Hugh Luke called Slote "a cosmopolitan of the imagination, who found or made her home place in Lincoln" (Spring/Summer 1981).*

Grandfather

Remembering Holland, by night he wrote
Where the lilac wind came through the bloom
And flared the smoke of the amber lamp.
My grandfather wrote in a still room.

He loved the shape of a thought seen.
Loved words: the body in sound, the bare
And sudden sharpness rounded sweet,
Like odor of grapes in a gold air.
Loved the page with words grown black
As pattern of twigs on prairie snow,
The swift mind clear as a wildbird wedge
In the cloud, in the sky's timeless flow.

Alone with the lone scratch of pen,
The sputter of flame, I think he heard
The wind-wheels turning, ever Delft,
And creaking low in a Holland word –
He wrote of God and the good church,
Organ rolling under the bells
In streets of starch; the fog down
From a hanging sea; the long canals
Of moon-ice ringing to silver stroke;
And peppernuts flung at Nikolas' door –

I think it was so, but no one read
That book of the old man's private store.
He burned each word, and then at last
He lay in a white unwritten bed.
The great wheels stopped on a winter hill,
And ice recovered whatever he said.
Black ice covered his mouth . . . and still,
Here I write where the green days bloom,
In a lilac wind, in a still room.

Weldon Kees
(1914–1955)

Born in Beatrice and educated at the University of Nebraska, Kees became a modernist polymath by the 1940s – poet, novelist, short-story writer, literary critic, playwright, painter, jazz pianist, and filmmaker – acquainted with the important literati of New York and San Francisco. In his preface to Kees's Collected Poems *(1960), Donald Justice calls Kees "among the three or four best [poets] of his generation," a generation that included Elizabeth Bishop, John Berryman, William Stafford, and Robert Lowell.*

For My Daughter*

Looking into my daughter's eyes I read
   Beneath the innocence of morning flesh
Concealed, hintings of death she does not heed.
   Coldest of winds have blown this hair, and mesh
Of seaweed snarled these miniatures of hands;
   The night's slow poison, tolerant and bland,
Has moved her blood. Parched years that I have seen
   That may be hers appear: foul, lingering
Death in certain war, the slim legs green.
   Or, fed on hate, she relishes the sting
Of others' agony; perhaps the cruel
   Bride of a syphilitic or a fool.
These speculations sour in the sun.
   I have no daughter. I desire none.

Dynamite for Operas

After the red rugs of the palaces,
Roofs of those great hotels, views of the sea,
I seem to be back in this familiar room again.
Brought here, perhaps. It was February when I left.

* Grace Bauer writes, "Nebraskans don't seem to embrace Kees the way they do other native sons (and daughters), but Kees – the Renaissance man of Beatrice is, in my view, worth embracing. His poems are often dark – even bleak – as is certainly true of this poem, but also powerful. The final couplet for me is like a kick in the gut. I was so fascinated by this poem, I wrote a response from the daughter's point of view." (*Editor's note*: See Bauer's "Note from the Imaginary Daughter," page 197.)

It is hard to touch death while part-time roles
In melodramas of decay provide the time
For one to smile eccentrically in dressing rooms.
I never smiled much here. Farewell, colleagues of the sublime!
I greet the welcome papers blowing down a street
I know too well. Someone has wound the clock,
Which ticks like a bomb, and is not culpable.

To wake again and know that time
Grinds on, grinds on, is what I missed,
Or so the blowing curtains seem to say.
That emptiness was richer than this emptiness.
Too rich. I liked it all the less for that.
A chilly landscape tightens up the mind.

Poem Instead of a Letter

Grasping at nothing in a swirl of leaves
Here in this smoky-faced and ruined town,
I think of you, across the continent,
Testing your smile that ripened in catastrophe
And wonderfully ready now for death.

The threadbare promise of our heritage
Is habit now; that other year turned winter
As we watched the fragments of a world
Dropping to pieces like a sick bouquet,
Missing the odor, though we named the time
Sufficiently. We know that odor now,
I think, as well as it is safe to know.
And even as I climb the steps, wishing you luck,
It fills the porches and the streets, while this rank wind
Blows through your rooms, untenanted.

What ranker winds may blow one cannot say,
Nor guess. The one tonight blows through the mind,
And every syllable is false, and dry.
Goodnight, goodnight. To strangers, to an empty street.

1926

The porchlight coming on again,
Early November, the dead leaves
Raked in piles, the wicker swing
Creaking. Across the lots
A phonograph is playing *Ja-Da*.

An orange moon. I see the lives
Of neighbors, mapped and marred
Like all the wars ahead, and R.
Insane, B. with his throat cut,
Fifteen years from now, in Omaha.

I did not know them then.
My airedale scratches at the door.
And I am back from seeing Milton Sills
And Doris Kenyon. Twelve years old.
The porchlight coming on again.

Small Prayer

Change, move, dead clock, that this fresh day
May break with dazzling light to these sick eyes.
Burn, glare, old sun, so long unseen,
That time may find its sound again, and cleanse
What ever it is that a wound remembers
After the healing ends.

James A. Emanuel
(1921–2013)

In Whole Grain *(1991), his collected poems, Emanuel doesn't mention being born in Alliance, Nebraska, only "a varied youth in contrasting areas of the country, foreign service as an infantry staff sergeant, a PhD from Columbia University, and university professorships in New York, France, and Poland," the latter in conjunction with his decision to move permanently to Europe in 1984. As a scholar, beginning with his 1967 book on Langston Hughes, Emanuel is credited with helping African American literature gain broad acceptance in the academy.*

Negritude

Black is the first nail I ever stepped on;
Black the hand that dried my tears.
Black is the first old man I ever noticed;
Black the burden of his years.

Black is waiting in the darkness;
Black the ground where hoods have lain.
Black is the sorrow-misted story;
Black the brotherhood of pain.

Black is a quiet iron door;
Black the path that leads behind.
Black is a detour through the years;
Black the diary of the mind.

Black is Gabriel Prosser's knuckles;
Black Sojourner's naked breast.
Black is a schoolgirl's breathless mother;
Black her child who led the rest.

Black is the purring of a motor;
Black the foot when the light turns green.
Black is last year's dusty paper;
Black the headlines yet unseen.

Black is a burden bravely chanted:
Black cross of sweat for a nation's rise.
Black is a boy who knows his heroes;
Black the way a hero dies.

Black Poet on the Firing Range

Cantcha pull that trigger?
sweat n yr eyes
done wet yr mind?
yaint sure yr mamas knees
scrubbed miles
her folded hands ironed mountains
her love all pennypinched and slow?
cant swallow all the blood
yr daddy iced beneath s heart
dammed till he thawed on you
when you showed brave
and Blackness in yr mind
set like a star?

Dont wanta take a hand
in whos to live and whos to die?
dont wanta join th game they played
on yr mamas stomach an yr daddys back?

If you too tender
if you cant shoot Budweiser
tween th eyes
bust Coca Cola off a tree
bull's-eye a Dixie cup

still . . . guess you hard, poet,
shootin from th hip
gettin' off bullets cant be heard
till they hit Whitey's mind
while he sittin sippin
readin nigger news

(saw im flinch in s chair
as if he lookin down a gun barrel
while he samplin you).

Go head, Black on –
guess trigger time for real
dont make
no noise

William Kloefkorn

(1932–2011)

William Kloefkorn, named Nebraska State Poet in 1982, was the author of numerous verse collections, including Swallowing the Soap: New and Selected Poems *(2010), as well as four book-length memoirs and two story collections. For many years, he was professor of English at Nebraska Wesleyan University. In addition to his many literary honors, he won first place in the 1978 Nebraska Hog-Calling Championship.*

Out-and-Down Pattern*

for John

My young son pushes a football into my stomach
and tells me that he is going to run
an out-and-down pattern,
and before I can check the signals
already he is halfway across the front lawn,
approaching the year-old mountain ash,
and I turn the football slowly in my hands,
my fingers like tentacles
exploring the seams,
searching out the lacing,
and by the time I have the ball positioned
just so against the grain-tight leather,
he has made his cut downfield
and is now well beyond the mountain ash,
approaching the linden,
and I pump my arm once, then once again,
and let fire.

The ball in a high arc
rises up and out and over the linden,
up and out over the figure
that has now crossed the street
that is now all the way to Leighton Avenue,

* Don Welch writes, "Long after the glories of Nebraska football fade, this remarkable poem will keep its head up. Never has a football been better used in Nebraska."

now far beyond,
the arms outstretched,
the head as I remember it
turned back, as I remember it
the small voice calling.

And the ball at the height of its high arc
begins now to drift,
to float as if weightless
atop the streetlights and the trees,
becoming at last that first bright star in the west.

Late into an early morning
I stand on the front porch,
looking into my hands.

My son is gone.

The berries on the mountain ash
are bursting red this year,
and on the linden
blossoms spread like children.

My Love for All Things Warm and Breathing*

I have seldom loved more than one thing at a time,
yet this morning I feel myself expanding, each
part of me soft and glandular, and under my skin
is room enough now for the loving of many things,
and all of them at once, these students especially,
not only the girl in the yellow sweater, whose
name, Laura Buxton, is somehow the girl herself,
Laura for the coy green mellowing eyes, Buxton
for all the rest, but also the simple girl in blue
in the back row, her mouth sad beyond all reasonable
inducements, and the boy with the weight problem,
his teeth at work even now on his lower lip, and

* Marge Saiser writes, "This poem resonates with me because it deals with a love of students, and it does so with specifics and intelligence. This poem could be a theme song for teachers."

the grand profusion of hair and nails and hands and
legs and tongues and thighs and fingertips and
wrists and throats, yes, of throats especially,
throats through which passes the breath that joins
the air that enters through these ancient windows,
that exits, that takes with it my own breath, inside
this room just now my love for all things warm and
breathing, that lifts it high to scatter it fine and
enormous into the trees and the grass, into the heat
beneath the earth beneath the stone, into the
boundless lust of all things bound but gathering.

At Bryan LGH–East in Lincoln, Nebraska

Dressed in a blue shirt and matching trousers, smiling
and dimpled, she floats into the room and, pausing
at the foot of the bed, raises her arms to form a V.
I am the Queen of Hygiene, she announces, sweetly,
and who in his right mind could resist?

For the past two days I have refused to bathe. But
now the urge to comply overwhelms the urge
to object. I am putty in the palm of the Queen.
Already I have been eased out of bed, out of my
gown and into the shower where I sit on a plastic

chair as the Queen of Hygiene soaps and rinses
her subject from head to foot, no quarter asked
or given, after which, with a thick warm towel,
she dries him, then helps him up and out
of the shower and into the gown and, ever so

slowly, back onto the bed where, his torso some-
what elevated, he closes his eyes and decides, this
time without much hesitation, to go on breathing.

On a table at my left lies the razor I'll use to smooth
my face for the lotion my wife, the Queen of Olfaction,
will deliver. Old Spice, a brand new bottle. In memory
of my father, she'll explain, splashing a liberal portion
on my cheeks and chin. Remember?

I remember. Her father, wherever he went, introduced
himself from half a mile away with the fragrance
of Old Spice. Another reason to love the Queen
of Olfaction: she can't stop loving her father.

✵

Two hours after midnight I am wakened by a soft voice
I recognize as Emily's. She wants permission
to draw four small vials of my blood. Help yourself, I
say. There's plenty more where those'll come from.
She tells me, as always, to guard my eyes; she's about

to turn on one of the lights. Emily. Chubby, polite,
efficient Emily – and gentle. Gently she slaps my arm,
locates a vein, gently injects a needle, having warned
me, gently, that I am about to feel a little sting. Emily.
The Queen of Phlebotomy. When the vials are filled

and labeled, I catch her eye. Emily, I say, but then
I don't say anything. She is dressed in absolute white.
In her right hand she is holding my dark red blood. Before
I can say what I neglected to say, the light
has gone out and with it Emily.

✵

Between two white sheets I lie warm and comfortable
and aromatic – and clean to the brink of godliness.
And though Emily closed the door behind her, I can hear
muted clicks and beeps and shuffles and words, each
sound a fact of existence, each silence a premonition.

My Granddaughter, Alyssa

Lovely in her persistence
she moves cross-country over a vast expanse
of well-tended prairie, thick ryegrass and fescue
clipped evenly and close, the path she and the others follow
lined with oak and ash, maple

and hackberry, each limb a string
on an instrument the west wind, warm and rising,
seems to be playing, and today it is *La Cinquantaine,*
the piece my granddaughter performed at a recent recital,
she standing stately and composed,

lovely in her self-assurance,
Alpine spruce against a hollow of neck and chin,
La Cinquantaine on a stand before her, notes from
the pages finding their way into the hands of the virtuoso,
into the fingers, into the tipends

that work the bow and the strings,
tipends that tonight will turn the pages of yet
another far-ranging book, my granddaughter lovely
in her patience, her good-natured thirst for understanding,
under her feet now a path

that dips and rises and fades, and
when she disappears around a distant bend
you turn to watch that space where you trust she'll
reappear, and soon enough there she is, proof that faith
can be more than a concept,

her legs picking up the pace as she
approaches the long uphill stretch to the finish
where multiple rows of onlookers stand waving and
cheering, and where a clock with its large red numbers
decrees an opus entirely its own – time,

like all who are up against it, moving on.

Don Welch

(1932–2016)

Don Welch, an award-winning teacher and poet, was born in Hastings, Nebraska. After living in Texas, Maryland, Illinois, and Colorado, he returned to teach for fifty years at the University of Nebraska at Kearney in the English and Philosophy departments, holding the first two endowed positions at that institution. He lived with his wife, Marcia, in Kearney and raced pigeons for most of his life. Homing, *his collected poems, appeard posthumously.*

Nebraska

Going west when the sun is going down,
following the highways like light cords.

❊

If Nebraska were the name of a Russian woman,
they could love her.
There would be a certain large-boned beauty about her.
Or she would be dressed in black and lace.
Her waist would be small,
and she would drag her long dress over a floor
into a study lined with French books.

She would be a pawn in huge novels of war.

❊

As it is, she is a woman of spare beauty.

❊

Turning away from him so that the fine hollows
of her back were toward the bed,
she said, Why do you do this to me?

Why do you keep imagining me in other
places and states?

And why do you keep assuming our children
are unhappy?

When Memory Gives Dust a Face

When dust like flour sifted the road,
and weeds were skeletal corsages;
when horses broke their hooves unshod
with careless grass their only forage,

she sang high songs. And we listened
as we walked to town. No voice
was more enriched by pain. Her tongue
cleaved to love to make it new.

In loss the dust assumed her songs.
And clods assumed they had been sung to.

Requiem for a Teacher

Not everyone can be informed by love,
nor every word worn and measured by grief's tongue.
In loss the shoulders of the blackbirds are our sum.

Yet if flight is song,
the cranes will come again to tell us what wing is,
and canaries bless our cottonwoods.

❊

It only takes two steps to make a rhythm,
one ear to hear a song;
and dumb by love, a mouth to find its way.

❊

You loved good works because they cleansed
the air between them.
The air for you was such a generous house.

❊

In absolute light are the hard still puzzled by soft ways?
Like the wise, do they know what to give into?
Graceless, what is their rhythm?

How many souls make up the inexhaustible winds?
How many of them taught with their bones' chalk?
What are the givens?

❋

Now the river bends in the curves of its dark arms.
Wherever its deeper currents run, the wind is weeping light,
and the evening catches on whatever waves.

❋

Is death that breath we hold inside ourselves until
it lips into the sun?
Like love, does it take us to the edge, and just beyond?
A line of cranes in its ellipsis?

❋

Morning. The river runs, and with it the incoherence of its foam.
As light burnishes everything you loved,
your shadow, smokeless, stays upon our tongues.

When That Snow Died

That night when the snow fell
there were so many white voices

each with the newness of genius each
an elf-flake on your lashes

Young how could we have known that the cold
could be more than Siberian

or that in the heart of the snow there was
an inaudible weeping

How I loved you your face turned upward
freckled with white

How I loved you when a million white words
were making sense of that lawn

It was like this when that snow died
lace burned

Nancy McCleery

(1933–)

Nancy McCleery's poetry has appeared in six book-length collections and numerous anthologies and journals. She received an MA from the University of Nebraska and has worked as a teacher and mentor principally in Nebraska, Alaska, and Missouri. She is known for her collaborations with visual artists, dancers, and musicians in producing her works for the stage, and her librettos have been performed internationally. A Gift from the River, *her collaboration with composer Robert Walters, was performed in 2005 with lead singers from the Metropolitan Opera and the University of Nebraska School of Music.*

"Everything Keeps Me Here, the Swallow"

writes Colette, "does not know
that it will leave in autumn.
Why would I surpass in wisdom
the most migratory of birds."

Anywhere it hangs its nest
on eaves, it leaves.
On the sun of its breast
it goes from cold weather.
Cardinal stays the winter
with sparrow; but you, swallow,
your song gone everywhere
in dawn down chimneys,
under the roofs of our barns,
our houses.

We scud in the dark,
worry that we seem to stay.
Our eyes glint for our misplaced spaces,
though with every step
we would lift off.

At dusk your flight
signals that we are close,
almost there,
or should be gone.

Family on the Platte

The wild grape and Mother
took my father's eye around the bend
thinking the kitchen, the boiling blue juice.
She looked through shallow water
for green stones, glints

of mica, sky, other rivers.
A long distance, World War II.
My brother shot toads with a BB gun.
I waded to a dry branch.
The grass whistled.

At sunset we met on a sandbar
to study the fire.
Now, in another state,
when sun diminishes
I sense cool air

coming through the willows.
I see us there,
feet still in the warm sand,
Dad's hands full of purple fruit.
But Mother, alone in her garden,

tends resurrection lilies, peonies.
ferns. Two brothers, thousands of ideas,
miles away. And my eyes
accepting oceans, rain.
No more words.

Girl Talk (music / purity)

Told me I could develop my writing by playing
the piano again. Told me: *Music, the purest*
of all art forms.

I was thinking not purity
but heart speaking to heart as in Beethoven,
as in the Blues, as in Thelonious Monk.

You had a good start, she blurted out,

then you moved down a rung or two
to slippery words gave up the piano.

I asked, Perhaps mantras – wouldn't that be
more pure? And what about love poems.
Told her the love poem may be talking
to itself alone. Maybe all poetry
does that, for the music of it.

She spouted how about playin' this upright
just a little bit of Mozart Bach?
Try playin' the piano again 'n then
just lay the music out there in poems
don't try to mean somethin' just present it
the way music 'n my sketches do
that's purity the reader finds the meanin'.

Told her you really tick me off when you harp
on music and lecture me on aesthetics
I already know. Besides, we don't
see things as they are anyway;

we see things the way *we* are. So do you
want Dame Edith Sitwell's "Façade"?

It was no use debating, trying to convince her
I wouldn't play her piano – a waste
of words, so I began studying another
of her AIDS quilt panels. She was stenciling
children's names on it, the many names.

Shirley Buettner
(1934–2008)

Born in Kansas, Shirley Buettner lived in Kearney, Nebraska, for over sixty years, where she taught writing for UNK's Department of English. In her later years she hosted monthly "Poetry with Shirley" gatherings, at which she read her own poems and those of other Nebraska poets. The author of Walking Out the Dark *(1984) and* Thorns *(1995), her poems appeared in anthologies and small-press publications, including* Prairie Schooner, Kansas Quarterly, Cottonwood Review, Pacific Review, *and* Abraxas. *Two of her poems also appeared in the national* American Life in Poetry *newspaper column, a weekly series created by Ted Kooser.*

Only the Doe Remains Voiceless*

After thrashing rain,
a stunned dusk, an absence
of sound, then presence,
a doe browsing brome
below the house.

She moves amid awakening
mummery: chortle of warblers,
burr of drenched beetles,
the numbing mosquito drill.
By the cave, toads rustle,
their night mounds growing
slick and black
before moonbreak.

Only the doe
remains voiceless,
leans over her heart,
a Ruth gleaning grain.
She nears the cave
where one mislaid sandal,
like an offering from Boaz,
swells with promise and rain.

* Don Welch writes, "Shirley was unique in her poetry because she wrote with such emotion as well as good description. She was as sensitive as she was gritty. Truthfully, I don't know a Nebraska woman poet who was as hands-on as she, and she makes us feel it."

The dark covers us
with a corner of its blanket.
Sensing my breathing
behind hushed lace,
the doe leaps to the river.

With the doe I send one vow
I bend to, for I,
after twenty years,
keep a similar silence.

Stillborn

He was as big
as an eight-year-old boy,
with long legs
and white eyelashes, thick
and creamy with sleep.

The farmer blew in his mouth,
and I pounded one side
of the chest where I thought
the heart was, jarring
the gelatin body.

With knees in the snow
we both leaned close
to the just-born brown whorls,
looking for a quiver,
and behind us
the black heifer mother
poured out a rainbowed placenta,
steaming, melting
the wind-hardened crust.

The Swiss Chalet Barometer*

for twenty years
they have not spoken
to one another

on sunny days
she shuffles across the threshold
to water her window boxes
and he sulks inside
by the chimney

when the weather worsens
she sits in her dim kitchen
singing her song
to no one
while he stands raging
on the doorstep

so it is with one marriage
half-lives in a dark house.

Neighbor

By July the fields frame
my neighbor across the west section.

Her windows, so carefully windexed,
flare and wink at me,

and from my back stoop I can see her
bent over her bean rows hoeing in

the night moisture. Soon the corn
throws up its green walls

---

* Ted Kooser writes, "Shirley Buettner wrote a number of fine poems before her death, and this is one I'm especially fond of for its ability to let the details convey the message. Poems like this teach us how to notice things."

covering the dark mouth of her house,
the nose, the eyes, and finally

the pale square hair of the roof.
Her wash flaps tearfully,

white handkerchiefs waving
goodbye, goodbye.

In Cottonwood Township

Saturday night in Cottonwood Township:
milkweed fluff floats the moted dusk.
I pull a loose thread from my jeans
and the back pocket falls off.
This is the way of the township,
a loosening, then a loss.

A raveling thread of geese glides Cottonwood Township.
The river, like a sign on a beckoning inn,
blinks on and off. Sunday
a daughter leaves for the city.
This is the way of the township,
a loosening, then a loss.

I gather milkweed pods, empty as cradles.
Painted, they glue into bright, brittle angels.
As I torch the ditch,
other pods snap, then vanish.
This is the way
of the township – a loosening,
then a loss.

Glenna Luschei

(1934–)

Born in Iowa, Glenna Luschei was educated primarily at the University of Nebraska (BA, BS, and MA degrees), with her PhD from the University of California at Santa Barbara. Luschei is the author of The Sky Is Shooting Blue Arrows *(University of New Mexico Press, 2014). She has published Solo Press books and magazines for fifty years. Her latest book is* Zen Duende, *a collaboration with Eric Greinke (Presa Press, 2015). Once a corn detasseler in Iowa, she is now an avocado rancher in Central Coast California.*

Startled to Wake

I smell my grandfather's coffee
and hear the hog futures
on the radio.

I smell the mash
grandmother spread
for the chickens.

It's nearly time to help
her gather the eggs.
It's nearly time to walk
with grandfather
to the post office.
We open the box for letters
unsettle the hen for chicks.

Now it's time for me
to write letters
to marry to bear
my own children.

It's autumn now.
Amazing to wake
still on this rapturous plane.
Not yet winter.

Larry Holland
(1938–1999)

Born, in his own words, "near the end of the Great Depression on the Kearney side of the Platte River," Larry Holland taught English and writing at Northeast Community College for twenty-six years. For many years he edited the Elkhorn Review *and, with Red Shuttleworth, hosted the first Nebraska Literature Festival in 1986. He considered his claim to fame "the fine and wonderful students he had over the years, in three high schools and one college." Holland died in a car accident in March 1999 while on his way to see the annual migration of the sandhill cranes, which he called "the long-throated disciples / of an uncertain season" ("Whether We Know or Not").*

Home School

Years before my father taught me to shoot
I watched Mom tie chickens by the legs
on the clothesline a dozen at a time.
With her stropped butcherknife
she'd move quick down the line
slicing beaked and wattled fruit,
never a drop of blood on her.
Neighbors preferred wringing necks,
bodies flopping headless about the yard.
She explained to me, never to them,
how flopping free bruises meat.

She scalded in a bucket, plucked,
gutted in the yard and carried
six-to-a-pan into the house,
birds to be singed over open flame
and scrubbed. Last, fast as a seamstress
could stitch shut a sliced thumb,
she'd clean the dozen hearts,
livers and gizzards. One day
she handed me the knife.

Years have left me to puzzle
how some have come vaguely to think

real pillows and comforters are stuffed
with the gutless stuffing of hollofil,
how gizzards grow in clumps
on styrofoam, and fowl
hatch frozen in plastic sacks.
I've been marked for life,
a warm Sunday-after-dinner feeling
that my mother taught me
sharp knives and small matters,
like giblets.

The Whisper of Bones Grating

for Barbara and Bob

Dragging tumors and blindness like loose cargo
enough to founder a freighter on a reef,
from greying muzzle to hindquarters
that can't keep up with the rest of her,
the Springer has passed her good days.
I help her into the pickup cab
she made in one hop last fall.
Then she sat on the seat
watching, anxious for fields and fencerows.
Now she lies on the floor.
I shove a twenty-two in my belt,
put a shovel in the back.

Off the road I lift her out.
She makes the shallow ditch and waits for me
to lift the bottom fence wire.
She heels a straight unsteady line
the half mile of cedar and ash shelterbelt.
The shovel carries heavy as eleven years must
on an old dog pointing the last scent.

I jab the shovel in the ground,
punctuation to whispers of the wind and cedar.
Ash leaves brittle as the season
make a sound like bones grating.

Fredrick Zydek

(1938–2016)

Fredrick Zydek was the author of ten collections of poems, three novels, a biography of Charles Taze Russell, and numerous articles, reviews, and essays. Born and raised in Buckley, Washington, he taught at the University of Nebraska Omaha and later at the College of Saint Mary. After retiring, he continued writing while dividing his time between his home in Omaha and a farm in Brunswick, Nebraska.

Nebraska Quartet

for Jim Kelly

I. Spring

Once more green creeps out on the branches;
everything with urges goes to the stems.
Nebraska grows wild and feathery – a thing
young in the eyes, crazed by fire, dizzy
with shoots of peony and grasses. The magic
of green magic is everywhere flaunting
its delicious stuff, and on the leaf, music.

II. Summer

Three o'clock hangs limp on the lawn. The leaves,
wide-eyed and full of wonder, stare into the sun
until, at last, they stare the damn thing down.
A few have already given the wind its way with them.
They swarm like butterflies, single-winged and full
of varicolored and dappled worry. I go among their
verdant music more exhausted than ashamed.

III. Autumn

Autumn confesses both stamen and stem with what
ails her. She wears too much makeup, begins
tinting her hair red, pulls the old shawl closer

on her shoulders, wears small aprons embroidered
in yellow and gold, sleeps in on Saturday
and sometimes arrives late for services wearing
old ribbons and bits of rag in her hair.

IV. Winter

Nebraska becomes one chunk of white glass,
chills the life from everything, reflects it
back along the Platte and Ogallala. A white-laced
spinster in gossamer gown walks slowly every inch
of the state, carries a single message to each
of them, recites their names, one leaf at a time.

Star Watching

The night is open to the stars.
I'm clinging to the planet
lost in whole flocks of them.
Enormous sprays of light
glisten across the long-domed sky
like ideas jump-starting
along the sinus of some great mind.
Some flutter in their places
like the pulse of frail things
at the edge of cold waters.
A few, constant as the seasons,
blink their red and platinum codes
through the milieu of time,
rich in what I hope to know of them.
How proud I am to walk among such stars,
to watch them carve out
their bright pastimes,
sure as the urges that conceive us.
Tonight, whole clumps of them
want me to know I'm the way
stars contemplate themselves.

Hilda Raz

(1938–)

Hilda Raz is Luschei Professor of English and Women's and Gender Studies, emerita, at the University of Nebraska. She was the fifth editor of Prairie Schooner. *Her books include poetry, essays, criticism, and anthologies, and her work has been widely published in journals and by Wesleyan University Press, Persea Books, the University of Nebraska Press, and elsewhere. Now the editor of an endowed poetry series at the University of New Mexico Press, she is also poetry editor of* Bosque *magazine.*

Diction

"God is in the details,"
I tell the kids
in the public school
at Milligan, Nebraska.
They wonder what I mean.
I tell them to look
out the window
at the spring fields
the mud coming up
just to the knee
of the small pig
in the far pasture.
They tell me
it's not a knee
but a hock
and I hadn't ought
to say things I know
nothing about. I say
the light on the mud
is pure chalcedony.
They say the mud
killed two cows
over the weekend.
I tell them the pig
is alive and the spring
trees are standing in a green haze.

They tell me school is out
in a week and they have to plant.
The grain elevator at the end
of Main Street stretches out
her blue arms. The kids say chutes.

Fast Car on Nebraska I-80: Visiting Teacher

Early sun on fields.
A pheasant flushes and skims
the north ditch on air.
Students, I say out loud, rehearsing
in the car, *this morning*
our subject is nouns,
how to pin them down.
Gold is the color of freedom,
I say, *the fields Mennonites farm*
to yield more than an acre can.

Later, the most compelling noun
is *car,* fast skimming away from a class
I've asked to describe death
in terms of silk tatters, the smoking gun, for example,
of a brother shooting over his sister's head.

The girl in the front row
who daubed her eyelids purple
wrote about *the-one-who-is-gone,*
meaning her sister. And wrote
about *the-one-who-did-it,*
meaning her brother who shot the gun,
whom she ought to hate – and doesn't.

She doesn't. She misses the black hair
of his head, his brown eyes, her sister's
pale skin, now gone *dead-white.*
I don't make her read out loud.

First thing they said, this is a Mennonite community
and a boy killed his sister here two weeks ago.
But they forgot to mention the family, the other kids in school.

Early Monday, driving through wet air at seven
I'd noticed the horizon did a good job
on my heavy mind: what had seemed a knot
so snarled I couldn't get a nail in
began to unwind as I watched through the windscreen.

Here, the town is groomed, each stubble lawn smooth
in a yellow fallow. The houses are brick.
Each child in grades two through twelve
is clean and well-dressed. Some seniors
they tell me in class, drive Thunderbirds,
or go visit China in the summer. In the library
I have a glassed-in office usually reserved
for the Monday–Wednesday speech teacher.
I work undisturbed. Nowhere here
is violence I can see, only the peace of community.

Not here, or in the deep ditches where pheasant harbor
or the deer. Who couldn't be happy here?

Prelude

We bring to our booth
pages packed full
of subject and verve
blood and tissue, the nutshells
of her history sharp under her elbow
as she leans hard, the full weight
of her language on this vision
or that one, and take in
the full length of our throats
swallowing, breathing air
we share with fifty others,
the smells of ripening toast

in the chrome slots, and we breathe out
tone, shading, the shouts necessary
for our Monday morning before light
streaks the sky, before the curtains close
against the glare for patrons in the next booth,
and the whole world opens . . .

For weeks, staticy news over the sink
as each night at the open refrigerator
I transport, unwrap, scrub, pare
and transform food for the family body.

Oh, Child-God who pushes
across the glass table top
the sharp clatter, the ruckus of our lives
blocks of Legos, steel gas tubes
torn across at the throat by some
torque from a machine too terrible
to posit now, at this table rinsed
by the kind and disinfectant cloth . . .

Trained by custom to serve
I set down the burden of dinner
wash my hands and begin to eat

the only possibility, finally,
turning away from the heat
reliable torque of hip socket
and ribs allowing the swivel
my body makes to sit down
or reach for the phone, gut
courage, to climb on the plane,

transfer, hoisting luggage
into the overhead bins, and arrive
at your side, child, in time
for your long surgery to come tomorrow
and I'll be there, your mother, where I belong
the old miracle of your birth belief enough
to see us through cut and clamp, the blood price

I signed to pay, and will, and will myself
onto the plane with books and cash, pastilles,
ribbons, cashmere socks, spare eyeglasses
and ribs, hip bones, reliable bone sockets, and
every recipe intact or documented, soft sacs bathed,
reliable tongue tucked up into the silence broken
by only one word, love, one phrase, you can, one other,
I'm here, child, your absolute company
as you are changed – radically – from one thing to another.*

* Jim Cihlar writes, " 'I'm here, child, your absolute company / as you are changed.' Hilda Raz walks a line of honesty with a skill informed by years of discipline as the longtime editor for *Prairie Schooner.*"

Ted Kooser
(1939–)

Ted Kooser was born in Ames, Iowa, and for many years worked at a desk in a Lincoln, Nebraska, insurance company. He was named U.S. Poet Laureate in 2004 and during his first term won the Pulitzer Prize in poetry. His most recent books are Splitting an Order *(poems), from Copper Canyon Press, and* The Wheeling Year *(prose vignettes) from the University of Nebraska Press. His third children's book,* The Bell in the Bridge *(Candlewick Press), was published in spring 2016.*

Etude

I have been watching a Great Blue Heron
fish in the cattails, easing ahead
with the stealth of a lover composing a letter,
the hungry words looping and blue
as they coil and uncoil, as they kiss and sting.

Let's say that he holds down an everyday job
in an office. His blue suit blends in.
Long days swim beneath the glass top
of his desk, each one alike. On the lip
of each morning, a bubble trembles.

No one has seen him there, writing a letter
to a woman he loves. His pencil is poised
in the air like the beak of a bird.
He would spear the whole world if he could,
toss it and swallow it live.

Screech Owl

All night each reedy whinny
from a bird no bigger than a heart
flies out of a tall black pine
and, in a breath, is taken away

by the stars. Yet, with small hope
from the center of darkness
it calls out again and again.

Pearl

Elkader, Iowa, a morning in March,
the Turkey River running brown and wrinkly
from a late spring snow in Minnesota,
a white two-story house on Mulberry Street,
windows flashing with sun, and I had come
a hundred miles to tell our cousin, Pearl,
that her childhood playmate, Vera, my mother
had died. I knocked and knocked at the door
with its lace-covered oval of glass, and at last
she came from the shadows and with one finger
hooked the curtain aside, peered into my face
through her spectacles, and held that pose,
a grainy family photograph that could have been
that of her mother. I called out, "Pearl,
it's Ted. It's Vera's boy," and my voice broke,
for it came to me, nearly sixty, I was still
my mother's boy, that boy for the rest of my life.

Pearl, at ninety, was one year older than Mother
and a widow for twenty years. She wore
a pale blue cardigan buttoned over a housedress,
and she shook my hand in the tentative way
of old women who rarely have hands to shake.
When I told her that Mother was gone, that she'd
died the evening before, she said she was sorry,
that "Vera wrote me a letter a while ago
to say she wasn't good." We went into the kitchen
and I sat at the table while she heated a pan
of water and made us cups of instant coffee.
She told me of a time when the two of them
were girls and crawled out onto the porch roof
to spy on my Aunt Mable and a suitor
who were swinging below. "We got so excited

we had to pee, and we couldn't wait, and peed
right there on the roof and it trickled down
over the edge and dripped in the bushes,
but Mabel and that fella never heard!"

We took our cups into her living room,
where stripes from the drawn blinds draped over
the World's Fair satin pillows. She took the couch
and I took a chain across from her. "I've had
some trouble with health myself," she said,
taking off her glasses and wiping them,
and I said she looked good, though, and she said,
"I've started seeing people who aren't here.
I know they're not real but I see them the same.
They come in the house and sit around
and never say a word. They keep their heads down
or cover their faces with cloths. I'm not afraid,
but I don't know what they want of me.
You won't be able to see, but one's right there
on the staircase where the light falls through
that window, a man in a light gray outfit."
I turned to look at the landing, where a patch
of light fell over the carpeted steps.
"Sometimes I think my Max is with them;
one seems to know his way around the house.
What bothers me, Ted, is that they've started
to write out lists of everything I own.
They go from room to room, three or four
at a time, picking up things and putting them back.
I've talked to Wilson, the chiropractor,
and he just says that maybe it's time for me
to go to the nursing home." I asked her
what her regular doctor said and she said
she didn't go there anymore, that "He's
not much good." "But surely there's medicine,"
I said, and she said, "Maybe so." And then
there was a pause that filled the room.

After a while we began to talk again,
of other things, and there were some stories
we laughed a little over, and I wept a little,

and then it was time for me to go, to drive
the long miles back, and she slowly walked me
to the door and took my hand again –
our warm bony hands among the light hands
of the shadows that reached to touch us
but drew back – and I cleared my throat and said
I hoped she'd take care of herself, and think
about seeing a real medical doctor,
and she said she'd give some thought to that,
and I took my hand from hers and waved goodbye
and the door closed, and behind the lace
the others stepped out of the stripes of light
and resumed their inventory, touching
the spoon I used and subtracting it from
the sum of the spoons in the kitchen drawer.

Sleep Apnea

Night after night, when I was a child,
I woke to the guttering candle
of my father's breath. It made a sound
like the starlings that sometimes
got caught in our chimney, a chirping
that would gradually, steadily build
to a desperate, flat slapping of wings,
then suddenly drop into silence,
into the thick soot at the bottom
of midnight. No silence was ever
so deep. And then, after maybe
a minute or two, I would hear
a twitter as he came to life again,
and could at last take a breath for myself,
a sip like a toast, lifting a chilled glass
of air, wishing us courage, those of us
lying awake through those hours,
my mother, my sister and I, who each night
listened to death kiss the fluttering lips
of my father, who slept through it all.

Martha Collins
(1940–)

Born in Omaha, Martha Collins has published eight books of poetry, including Admit One: An American Scrapbook *(Pittsburgh, 2016),* White Papers *(Pittsburgh, 2012), and the book-length poem* Blue Front *(Graywolf, 2006). She has also published four collections of co-translated Vietnamese poetry and edited two anthologies. Collins founded the creative writing program at UMass–Boston and served for ten years as Pauline Delaney Professor of Creative Writing at Oberlin College. She lives in Cambridge, Massachusetts.*

White Paper 24

The Irish were not, the Germans
were not, the Jews Italians Slavs and others
were not, or were not exactly or not quite
at various times in American history.

Before us the Greeks themselves
were not (though the weaker enemy
Persians were), the next-up Romans
themselves were not either.

And later the Europeans were not
until Linnaeus named by color,
red white yellow and black.

Even the English settlers were only
vaguely at first, to contrast with natives,
but then with Africans, more and more
of them slaves to be irreversibly,
totally different from, they were.

Then others were not, then were,
or were not, but gradually became,
leaving only, for a time, black
and yellow to be not.

Then there were other words
for those who were still or newly
(see *immigrant, Arab*) somehow not
the same and therefore not.

Thus history leaves us nothing
but not: like children playing at being
something, we made, we keep
making our whiteness up.

William Trowbridge
(1941–)

William Trowbridge's graphic chapbook, Oldguy: Superhero, *was published by Red Hen Press in spring 2016. His new full collection,* Vanishing Point, *is forthcoming from Red Hen in 2017. His other collections are* Put This On, Please: New and Selected Poems, Ship of Fool, The Complete Book of Kong, Flickers, O Paradise, *and* Enter Dark Stranger. *He teaches in the University of Nebraska MFA in Writing program and was Poet Laureate of Missouri from 2012 to 2016.*

Stark Weather

> . . . and it seem as though i could
> see ny heart before ny eyes, turning
> dark black with Hate of Rages, or
> harhequinade, stripped from that munner
> life leaving only naked being-Hate.
> – *Diary of Charles Starkweather*

On the Great Plains in March,
the wind blows for days.
Gutter pipes vibrate, shingles flap;
things begin to come loose.
Once they found old Miss Purdy
wandering at midnight on U.S. 40,
her dainty-laced nightgown billowing
over her spindly, blue-gray thighs.
It took three deputies to hold her down
till the doctor arrived.

On the Great Plains in March,
the dry elm scrapes
at an upstairs window,
dust devils swirl and disperse
across the wide, empty fields,
and a pistol shot sounds
no louder than a screen door
slapping on a porch.

Peony Park, Omaha

I got my first job there, where everyone in Omaha
came to cool off in the summer – 4-million-gallon pool,
like a small lake with a beach, high board, high tower,
plus indoor and outdoor ballrooms for the bands
coming through: Ellington, Kenton, Basie, Herman.
I flipped burgers in the refreshment stand, 85¢ an hour,
and mopped up after closing. Once a week, I helped
scoop back sand that had worked its way onto the bottom.
If we didn't, the water would look dirty. Every time,
we'd pull in an adult-sized turd or two. Blacks
were barred, since they were said to be unclean.
There were drownings and dumb accidents: a guy dove
off the tower with a swim mask on, which splintered
into his face. The 16 lifeguards for the 4th were too few
for the dead kid. Our crew ogled the girls in swimsuits,
how they'd reach down and tuck a shapely cheek
back under cover. The jockeys showed up Mondays,
horny little guys who carried knives and grudges.
When we got bored, which was frequently, we'd
mold ten pounds of burger into a meat-puppet head
and, from behind the grill partition, work its mouth
to rattle customers. Once, we tossed a handful into the fan
by the juke box, where the ducktailers liked to preen.
They'd played "Transfusion," by Nervous Norvus, 15 times.
They didn't dare retaliate, since our crew included four
bruisers who doubled as goon squad, hired to bum's-rush
troublemakers out the front gate. We held our own Olympics,
with events like who could carry the most cases of beer
up from the cellar at once (the goon squad always
took gold) or who could get the most burgers on the grill
at once. I broke the record with 120, scorched down
to silver-dollar size. In later years, the crowds kept shrinking,
even after blacks were allowed to swim. After the bankruptcy,
developers razed the place and built a mini-mall, leaving
half the front gate as "memento." But there's still
a Facebook page. Old-timers will tell you, tears welling,
how they grew up with the place – white ones, that is.

Roy Scheele

(1942–)

Born in Houston, Texas, Roy Scheele lived in New Orleans and Shreveport, Louisiana, before moving to Lincoln at the age of three. He was educated in Lincoln public and parochial schools and attended the University of Nebraska–Lincoln, where he studied under Karl Shapiro and took a BA in classical Greek and an MA in English. In 2013 he was one of three finalists for Nebraska State Poet. He has been Poet in Residence at Doane University in Crete, Nebraska, since 1990.

Tell Me Again

Tell me the story of the cranes again:
how they descend from several thousand feet
(up where the sun will show them on the wing
as if they were snow white and not light gray,
so that they flash then darken as they turn
and come down gliding with their wings outspread);
how when they land they stutter-step at first
and flap their wings and send the nearby birds
hopping and flapping to make room for them,
as if a stone'd been thrown into a pond
and a wave of feathers circled out from it;
tell me once again about the fields
whose harvest stubble makes them feel secure,
the fields they gather in and fatten on
before a month from now they're off again;
tell me about the Platte, their nurse and mother,
her sandbars where they shelter for the night,
the roiling, dimpled flows above her currents;
remind me once more of the sound they make,
steady as a chorus of spring frogs
or pigeons under rafters in a barn;
and how just once, the closest we have been,
we saw a male lean over and pick up
a shred of cornstalk, flip it to his head
and do a sort of jester's madcap dance,
leaping in place until our laughter spread
and he grew tired of such foolery:
tell me the story of the cranes again.

Home Stretch

She stood at fifteen hands when she began
(15, 2 to be exact), a two-year-old
chestnut with a blaze between her eyes,
but no one liked her chances in those days –
no one, that is, but Sames. He saw in her
the local champion she would become.
It was his enthusiasm that convinced
the other trainers right out of the gate,
and when she didn't lose a single race
that year, the public – well, they caught on too.
The odds kept tumbling as her earnings grew.

I guess the thing you'd notice about Sames –
he looked like he knew almost everything.
There was a kind of cocksure swagger to him,
and he endorsed this in the way he dressed,
wearing a different silk shirt every day,
the colors all as bright as racing silks.
One I remember in particular,
a sort of tangerine, so deep an orange
you'd swear that you could squeeze it for the juice.
He often wore a porkpie hat as well
and always chewed the stub of a cigar.
There in the half-light of the early dawn
I see him still, a figure in a frieze,
leaning against the top rail with one foot
upstirrup-like upon the lowest rail,
shouting, through a megaphone of hands,
instructions to the boy who worked her out.
He told me once, the first time he saw her
he noticed her economy of motion
and was impressed by it, but also saw
she had no tendency to drift out wide
(or if she did, he said, you'd hardly know it).
Funny how a trainer always sees
the thing or things that set a horse apart.
One time I saw him step back from the rail,
look down at his watch and simply smile.

That was the closest that he ever came
to telling me how high he rated her.

At first he ran her in the small-purse stakes
at little tracks around the area:
Lincoln, Fonner Park, and Madison,
then later at Ak-Sar-Ben, where one meet
she drew a stable berth beside the great
Who Doctor Who. It could be that success
rubs off, said Sames, and flashed that smile of his.
Myself, I think she didn't need such help.
She had it covered in that stride of hers
and her combativeness, her will to win.
None of the corners cut by other trainers,
especially on those small Nebraska tracks,
was ever used by Sames on any mount –
those whips, for instance, with an electric charge
that crack on contact with a horse's flesh.
He had a knack with horses. He would blow
into one's ear until it tensed and flickered,
then take its muzzle, turn its face to him,
stroke its forehead, look it in the eye.
Then soft, but firm, the way a father speaks
to a pouting child, he would speak to it
in measured tones, almost in cadences,
and usually the horse would settle down.
You had to see it, really, to believe it.

That's how he brought this horse of his along,
this filly apple-of-his-eye. Sames knew
she wasn't ready for the big time yet,
but he was working on her confidence,
believing he could make the horse believe.
He babied her with sugar cubes and apples
and told her what a handsome heart she had.
She'd look at him and seem to understand.

So: the next year, her second season out,
began just like the first; race after race
was hers. Mostly she'd lie just off the pace
and then make up the difference down the stretch.
One of the jocks who'd ridden other mounts

said he was always nervous in the lead.
He said she'd slip up on you just like that
when you were running clean, and just like that
was round you in a spray of mud or dust.
He said she was one hell of a good horse.
The pressure built, of course, as she kept winning,
and all that spring she did, into the summer.

And then at Prairie Meadows, near Des Moines,
maybe halfway through the meet: she had won
every race again, won them handily,
when one sweltering hot late afternoon
she went out as the odds-on favorite.
Sames later said that she was just as calm
as she could be, back there in the paddock,
under his hands and voice, and he had thought
that maybe she would run a special race.
As usual she hung back in the pack
until the far turn, when she made her move.
How fluidly she glided then, her easy strides
eating the sifted dirt beneath her hooves,
horse after horse erased behind her charge,
her jock up leaning forward featherlight
and all the slanted rail posts spinning by
as she swung wide and out into the lead,
when suddenly – oh, God! Sames caught his breath –
her right foreleg had crumpled and she fell
asprawl out to the side while her momentum
carried the jockey, leaning forward still,
into a sudden effigy of flight,
landing on his elbows, tumbling over,
breaking his clavicle as gravity caught up.
All *she* could do was raise her head against
the agony – a broken cannon bone.
Sames rode out with the vet, leaped from the van,
cradled the filly's head in his vast lap,
leaned over whispering into one ear
as the vet's hypodermic bit her flesh,
and then she shuddered wildly and was gone.
He stayed with her like that until the truck
came to cart her off with all his hopes.
That night he cried and cried – for both of them.

Donna Whitewing-Vandall

(1943–2012)

Donna Whitewing-Vandall (Winnebago Sioux) was born in Sutherland, Nebraska, and held degrees from the Institute of American Indian Arts in Santa Fe—where she studied drama, dance, and writing—and the University of Montana. An internationally published poet and playwright, she served as executive director of the Aberdeen Area Tribal Chairman's Health Board and as cultural liaison for the dean of Little Priest Tribal College in Winnebago, Nebraska. Her poems appear in The Whispering Wind: Poetry by Young American Indians *(1972),* Voices from Wah'Kon-Tah: Contemporary Poetry of Native Americans *(1974), and* Native American Literature *(1999).*

Love Song

Your being has caused
an indelible line
through the crimson shadows
of my past;
Over the silent
white and blue days;
Into,
Merging,
And finally blending
with the deep dark quiet
mountains
of my life.

August 24, 1963 – 1:00 A.M. – Omaha

Heavy breathing fills all my chamber
Sinister trucks prowl
down dim-lit alleyways.
Racing past each other,
cars toot obscenities.
Silence is crawling in open windows
smiling and warm.

Suddenly,
crickets and cockroaches
join in the madness:
cricking and crawling.
Here I am!
A portion of some murky design.
Writing,
because I cannot sleep,
because I could die here.

[Untitled]

Clustered moon doves
light the garden path
My heart scarcely beats
in time.

Marjorie Saiser
(1943–)

Born in Texas, Marjorie Saiser grew up along the Niobrara and Keya Paha rivers in Nebraska and earned a master's in creative writing from UNL, winning the Vreelands and Academy of American Poets awards. Her books have received the WILLA and four Nebraska Book awards. Saiser's poems are in Nimrod, Prairie Schooner, Cimarron, Chattahoochee Review, RHINO, Plainsongs, burntdistrict, American Life in Poetry, *and* The Writer's Almanac. *Her fifth full-length collection,* I Have Nothing to Say About Fire, *is from the Backwaters Press (2016).*

Luke Says It's Another Silly Idea

Me, wanting to show chickens at the fair
and he says I don't have enough

to do, wait until I have babies
to take care of, and of course he's

right. Still, my little banty
struts the yard every inch

a prizewinner, the way he lifts
each foot, places it, the way

his comb shakes and his eye
shines with intention. I could

strut like that, if things were different;
if things were different, I could

strut like that.
Luke says he doesn't know why

I want banties, a pair,
not worth the corn they eat. But I think

maybe there's a place for feathers and strut.
Even a tin can, from the right angle,

glints blue like a diamond in the road.
And the hen lays her eggs

which I boil and have for a second breakfast
when Luke is out of sight. Two of those

like a couple of white stones on a saucer,
my salt, my window, after he's gone,

before I do the dishes. I am
a blue ribbon rascal.

Pulling Up Beside My Husband at the Stoplight

We are going to the same place
but we have to take two cars.
Sunday morning and there's not much traffic
so I pull up beside him at the stoplight.
There he is in his car, beside my car,
his profile in the window, the brown of his hair.
He turns and blows me a kiss. I watch it
float on by. I motion for another.

I'm thinking how he comes to wake me
on any weekday morning,
the sound of his workboots across the carpet,
the scent of his face when he finds me in the covers,
kisses my eyebrow and the corner of my mouth,
tells me the weather report
and the precise time of day.

So I roll down the window of the car,
whistle in my throat, pull my glasses
crooked on my face, do my best baboon snorting,
pound the horn as if it were bread dough.
There is only the lady in the white Buick but he
is embarrassed, glad when the light turns green.
Me, I'm stepping on the gas, catching up,
planning what I can do at 56th and Calvert.

The Story, Part of It

The story, part of it, is that
the tractor was parked, running,
at the top of the hill, and
my sister Jennie, ten years old, climbed
up and took a seat at the wheel. The story,
part of it, is that my father worked on something
attached behind the tractor, the digger or the chain
perhaps; the story does not tell all. It tells
what he said to Jennie, his instruction; it tells
what he said into the fierce wind blowing that day,
the roar of the wind and the roar of the tractor.
He said *Whatever you do, don't step on the clutch.*
The wind took his words, flipped and turned them,
gusted them even as it gusted everything,
even as it tossed the ends of the red scarf Jennie wore,
flapping it out and back, out and back. Jennie
heard him say *Step on the clutch* and she did.
The tractor lurched down the hill like an animal
freed. The story, part of it, tells how the tractor
rolled, gaining, how Jennie stood steadfast
on the clutch, hanging onto the wheel, her hair
and her red scarf flying with the speed of it, how
the tractor sped down the slope until it
hit the barbed wire fence at the bottom,
broke through and rolled over,
how she flew off, and the clutch engaged and
killed the engine. Everything was at that second
silent from the roaring, and Jennie was
face down on the grass, alive, but he, my father,
thought she was dead.
And years later when my father was dying, I called
Jennie. *You'd better come,* I said. She arrived
at the hospital and I met her at the main door
to show her through the maze, the halls,
to my father's last room. We turned the turn
and could see him ahead. No longer
a man at work. Or rather a man doing

the new work of dying. He sat in the bed, tubes
into the skin of the backs of his hands.
He looked up and caught
sight of her, of us, and then he did what
Jennie cannot explain, get over, understand,
make sense of: he put his hand over his eyes;
he looked down at the floor while we came to him.
The story, part of it, is that Jennie cannot let go of this.
She told me: *It's what he's always done –*
he did not want to see me, to look at me.
No, I told her. *No, it was to keep from crying.*

Father*

his head for the first time lies on a satin pillow
they have trimmed his nails shorter than he ever did
but he would not mind
tolerant even now
of another man's way of doing things

his arm was larger, rounder
lying across the wheel
to guide the whining truck
three-quarters up the hill
the door open, the gravel of the road edge
and wet low bushes crawling by
he looking back at the trees and the trailer
saying calmly jump if we jack-knife
you'll be all right

his arms bulging under short sleeves rolled twice
his head resting against the wiry red hair of the cow
keeping the rhythm of the milk
cutting lines into the foam

---

* Greg Kuzma writes, "I first heard Marge read this on a short film in 1971 or '72 and never forgot it. She views her father in his casket and recalls key and pure moments they had together. A brief, understated poem, whose scenes blaze into memory. This man we would all be proud to know."

or on the scaffold against the new wall
lifting the concrete block, turning it,
fitting it into the pattern
tilting the blade of the trowel
tapping the block with the handle

his face is free of all the things he should have done
he should have bought his father's farm
he should have joined the union
he should have gone fishing in south carolina
with young eddie

but when the dirt falls on the curved polished lid
when it slides off the shovel
like a hand opening to let something go
everything will be all right
all things are as they should be

I would like to touch again
the rounding of his arm
put my fingers into the L of his elbow

cover his hand
as he showed me in Kramer's mortuary
that grandmother did not mind being touched
and that those dead, and living, are not untouchable
if you are not afraid.

Greg Kuzma

(1944–)

Born in Rome, New York, Greg Kuzma graduated from Syracuse University's writing program in 1967, then spent forty-two years teaching beginning poetry writing at the University of Nebraska, where he is currently professor emeritus. The author of thirty books and chapbooks, he contributed some 1,500 poems to journals between 1967 and 1979. He describes his recent books as "longish meditative and lyrical poems built around a narrative spine." Hose and Iron, *his selected poems, was published in spring 2017 by Stephen F. Austin State University Press. "Teaching writing," he says, "is the best thing I've done."*

The Tree

The one who planted this great tree,
as surely someone must have done,
so perfect-distanced from the house it is,
lives somewhat distant, unknown to me,
or else is dead, so old is the tree this year,
or else goes by each day in a car
and says, "Look at that tree,
I put it in the ground, a day
like this one, very wet,
my shoes, all mudded, sat
on the porch two days,
I thought that they would never dry."

An August Evening

My son's face in the mirror
all eyes and lashes, and warm
vulnerable flesh of cheeks,
mixed with the empty fields
behind his back he had
not looked into, understood,
or ever travelled. Last night
out riding in the car, top

down, the wind went through his
hair, ruffled it about
his eyes and ears the way
my wife in her great long love
takes his face in her
hands and brings it
near her own.

The Birds My Son Showed Me

The birds are asleep in the tree
in the front of the yard.
A large towering sort, greenish blue,
on which the snow hangs.
Under the thickest limbs
the sparrows and other small birds
perch for the night.
You can touch them, Mark says,
laying your hand
upon the undersides of them.
They are there to be taken,
helpless, weary from all their living.
In the day it is different.
There is all this business to be done.
Crossing and leaping up,
descending in swirls upon some fallen grain.
Or rising full of purpose and flight.
hustle, and an energy wild and yet tame
at the same time, keeping their distance,
setting some sort of obscure example.
But in the dark they are like ourselves,
confused and solitary, idle and withdrawn.

Michael Skau

(1944–)

Born in Chicago, Michael Skau taught English at the University of Nebraska at Omaha for thirty-seven years. He has published poems in Carolina Quarterly, Northwest Review, Paintbrush, Kansas Quarterly, Laurel Review, Passaic Review, Hawai'i Review, *and* Texas Review, *among many others. He was named winner of the 2013 William Kloefkorn Award for Excellence in Poetry, and his collection of poems,* Me & God, *was published by Wayne State College Press in 2014.*

Cranes

The sandhill cranes will soon return
to the braided river among the fields
of corn stubble and shifting sandbars.
They will gather in throngs or pairs, or some
will stand alone, among the grey
red-capped tens of thousands as they stretch
their wings in dance or bob to feed
on grain debris. At twilight, safe
from predators, on spindly legs,
they will tiptoe in raucous gawkiness
through shallow water and marshy sands.
I have traveled to the Platte three times,
once with two friends, both of them now
dead, twice with lovers who later left
me. Come March I shall drive there alone.

Freedom's Slaves

We were always getting lost in liberty.
Our whims would steer our steps toward marshy ground;
we'd slush on through rather than retreat, bound
and shackled by impulse as though by integrity
in stubborn determination not to appear
shallow or admit to being wrong. We chained
our wills to causes that dried our souls and drained
our spirits, chafed to discontent each career.
We gave our hearts to all the beasts that licked
our hands, then wondered why they'd turn and bite
or scratch us with ungrateful claws. We wooed
risk, and foolhardiness battered and kicked
our marriage to pulp, till good and bad and right
and wrong confused us into servitude.

Mary K. Stillwell
(1944–)

Born in Omaha, Mary K. Stillwell studied writing in New York with William Packard and on the plains with Ted Kooser. She earned her PhD in plains literature, has published widely, and co-edited Nebraska Presence, *an anthology of contemporary Nebraska poets (Backwaters). Her books include* Moving to Malibu *(Sandhills Press, 1989),* The Life and Poetry of Ted Kooser *(University of Nebraska Press, 2013),* Fallen Angels *(Finishing Line Press, 2013), and* Maps & Destinations *(SFA Press, 2014).*

A Waltz for My Mother

Wish I could lift that old gold and white Lira
from the plush red velvet of its case one more time,

guide the wide straps over my shoulders, right, then left,
adjust the bellows over my chest, unsnap the latches

that hold them closed, send the fingers of my left hand
in search of the rhinestone that marks the button C,

and those of my right to the keys to play,
one, two, three, what I called The Bernice Waltz,

to honor my mother on the anniversary of her birth.
Words and chords, notes and rests, all of them lost.

But not the honeysuckle, sounding its golden trumpets
even as the dew clings like tears to the spider's web.

Tonight, lightning bugs blink their songs onto staffs
strung like badminton nets across the lawn;

overhead and within, stars and chromosomes bow
to one another, dance my mother's ghost notes, one, two, three.

The Cutting

The sun has pulled
the dew from the grass,
leaving the roots warm, humid, soft.
The sky is blue, cloudless.
We wait for the breeze.
It comes.

The cutting begins.
I follow my stepfather:
my tractor after his.
The umbrella shades him,
vibrates above his head.
My tractor after his,
my circle inside the circle
of his mower, I trace
the boundary of his last round.
I follow the tire treads
with my eye,
change gears for the first
sharp turns, later follow
rounded corners.

Insects swirl from the grass.
The heat presses up
from the tractor.
The sun shines.
He leads.
I follow, cutting
farther and farther
into the field's center,
until one long swath remains.

He signals and turns to watch.
I circle and approach
as the mower lays the final
grass to rest.

R. F. McEwen
(1945–)

R. F. McEwen was born in Chicago, Illinois. Since 1962 he has been a professional logger and tree trimmer, and he has been teaching English in Chadron, Nebraska, since 1972. His work has appeared in numerous journals as well as The Yellow Nib: The Literary Journal of the Seamus Heaney Centre for Poetry. *His book* Heartwood *was featured on* CBS Sunday Morning. *He co-produced a two-CD collection of the great Irish* sean nos *singer Joe Heaney:* Tell a Story: Joe Heaney in the Pacific Northwest *(Camsco Music). His most recent book is* Casey Joe MacBride's White River, volume 1, *published by Stephen F. Austin State University Press.*

Stacking Rick Wood: Getting On

> *For as long as I was hauling firewood up to Clive Guildersleeve at Wounded Knee, South Dakota, he was selling it by the rick, which came out to about a fourth a cord, since most wood stoves back then couldn't handle much more'n a twelve–fourteen-inch piece of wood. Back here in Crown Point, Indiana, though, a sixteen-inch log will set up real nice in your fire place. So here a rick comes out to about one-third of a cord. It's different in a lot of places.*
> – Don Green; Crown Point, Indiana (1972)

My grandfather and Carlos Little Boy
were right that year the south White River froze
before its time; I think in late November,
nineteen sixty-three. And we'd been cutting
rick wood there, northeast of Chadron, six miles
off the Slim Buttes road; dead ash and elm
(and when my grandfather said "Ellum" we
just grinned). Those times we worked past dark we came
prepared with canvas for a lean-to deep
within the grove; then after dark we'd take
some beans and fry bread; coffee, too, and pie.

I couldn't cut then, but I'd rick the wood
and keep the saws in gas and oil, and sharp.
After my parents quit for good six years before,
my grandfather and Carlos Little Boy

kept me in line. We moved to Chadron and
I went to school almost every day.
Most weekends we worked yard jobs, cut rick wood;
most summers they both wrangled at Fort Rob
while I stayed back with my aunt Rose. I had
to keep my grades in school, my teachers pleased.
The winter I began this with, we'd worked
Thanksgiving break, then stayed the weekend through.
At night the wind pushed hard and had its say.
Upon their faces I could only catch
a sort of cross-cut flashing in the flames,
within their voices only floating bits
that seemed to hang upon the smoke and drift
into a limitless repose. I heard
them once again today, a decade and a half
gone by, on graduation day – I heard
my grandfather and Carlos Little Boy
intone this moment while the river froze.

John Early Remembers the Moment of His Wife's Death

He remembered that he'd walked out toward the strand
late afternoon to fetch a net and found
his grandfather abroad with several more,
their faces snared in lashings of dark weeds
that crossed the caverns where their eyes would be,
so that he had to touch his sleeve before
the old man caught the full of him and stepped
aside to kiss his cheek. Her sickness was
upon her five or seven days, but not
enough to hold him from the strand, or from
the sea itself, although those last two days
he'd kept to home and did what little bit
she might contrive until, late afternoon,
she'd had her cup, and he'd gone off to fetch the net.
Her glance upon him as he closed the gate
(he now imagined) would've coaxed him back
to say goodbye again. But when he met

his grandfather he knew that she was gone
because his grandfather was dead past forty years,
and all his boat were dead along with him
with not a one of them to find the shore.
On many nights to come John Early yearned
to resurrect that moment when he knew
his wife was dead, and feel the old man's lips
once more upon his cheek, unlearn his news.

Barbara Schmitz

(1945–)

Born in Omaha, Barbara Schmitz grew up where "the Platte and the Missouri rivers meet and kiss" and taught writing and literature at Northeast Community College for thirty years, founding the Visiting Writers series there. Two of her poetry books have won honors from the Nebraska Center for the Book. She recounts her spiritual search in the memoir Path of Lightning *(2012). She lives in Norfolk with Bob listening to the traffic on Highway 81, sometimes teaching writing in her attic. She is Malena's grandmother.*

Supper

I'm making a tuna casserole,
adding white and green noodles
to water boiling in a cast iron pan.
He's fixing the broken boards
in the fence. Our son's off playing.

I resist the urge to go to the back door,
storm glass still on,
and wave a movie wave
across the green grass, across
the theater, across eternity.

All the couples "forever
and ever, Amen" repeating
this scene, wearing these costumes
complete with opposite sets of genitals
as if they were real, and we existed,
he and I, in this time,
this old house, supper almost ready.

I Go to Hell

in my dream I go to hell
the whole room goes down
like an elevator
hell is an assembly line
people do things to you
but you don't have to take it
if you don't think you deserve it
they try to throw hot water on me
and torture my hands
no thanks I say turning away
my hair is up in rollers
I think I better take it down
because I will be there a long time
and it will be too curly
also my huge pearls break and I have to carry them
and the one roller I took out around in my hand
there's lots of smoky rooms
we come back up
awake in sleeping bags on the floor
I go to the bathroom
there are three toilets hooked together
oh I say Father Son & Holy Ghost

John Trudell

(1946–2015)

Born in Omaha, John Trudell grew up near the Santee Sioux Reservation in northern Nebraska, served in the U.S. Navy during the Vietnam War, and was a leading spokesman during the 1969 takeover of Alcatraz by a group known as the Indians of All Tribes. Trudell took part in the occupation of the Bureau of Indian Affairs in Washington, D.C., in 1972 and served as national chairman of the American Indian Movement during the 1970s. After a suspicious fire killed his pregnant wife, their three children, and his mother-in-law in 1979, Trudell turned to writing poetry, recording and performing music, and acting in film. The poems featured here served as song lyrics on his albums Bone Days *(2001) and* The Moremes *(2007), respectively.*

Crazy Horse

Crazy Horse
We hear what you say
One Earth one Mother
One does not sell the Earth
The people walk upon
We are the land
How do we sell our Mother
How do we sell the stars
How do we sell the air

Crazy Horse
We hear what you say
Too many people standing their ground
Standing the wrong ground
Predators face he possessed a race
Possession a war that doesn't end
Children of god feed on children of earth
These days people don't care for people
These days are the hardest
Material fields material harvest
Decoration on chain that binds
Mirrors gold the people lose their minds

Crazy Horse
We hear what you say
One Earth one Mother
One does not sell the Earth
The people walk upon
We are the land
Today is now and then
Dream smokes touch the clouds
On a day when death didn't die
Real world time tricks shadows lie
Red white perception deception
Predator tries civilizing us
But the tribes will not go without return
Genetic light from the other side
A song from the heart our hearts to give
The wild days the glory days live

Crazy Horse
We hear what you say
One Earth one Mother
One does not sell the Earth
The people walk upon
We are the land
How do we sell our Mother
How do we sell the stars
How do we sell the air

Crazy Horse
We hear what you say
Crazy Horse
We hear what you say
We are the seventh generation
We are the seventh generation

Cry Your Tears

Now you want us
To cry your tears for you
After we've already bled for you
Already been dead to you
Now you want us
To cry your tears for you

Chapters of a democracy story
Descendants of genocide
Twelve score and more years ago
We went from being the majority
To being the smallest minority
Now you want us
To cry your tears for you

We saw that emptying
Early morning skyline
Back through that horizon
Duck Valley 1979, Wounded Knee
Sand Creek, that Trail of Tears
Exactly how did our land
Become your country
Now you want us
To cry your tears for you
While we're still crying tears of our own

With your past as your future
That industrial ruling class
Using religion as a weapon
Distilling love into hate
Pointing fingers and name-calling evil
Sacrificing lives and blood
Making the innocent the new virgins
Offerings to the gods of profit
Now you want us
To cry your tears for you

In the homeland security
Pretending corporate corruption
Isn't economic terrorism
Money talks while the government listens
Compiling files on ones who think different
Conditioning an acceptance of debt
And not to expect the truth
So get used to hearing the lie
Now you want us
To cry your tears for you

Misusing the beauty
Turning freedom into a killing machine
Mass murdering the environment
Weaponizing the psychology of fear
And pushing material addiction with
A substitution of rules faking the law
The bill of rights becomes collateral damage
Making the constitution another broken treaty
Now you want us
To cry your tears for you

Way this story is unfolding
We may end up crying together
As in crying at the same time
But we're short on tears to cry for you
With all these tears to cry of our own
Now you want us
to cry your tears for you

Kathleene West
(1947–2013)

Born in Genoa, Nebraska, West grew up on the family farm, then graduated from UNL with a BA in English and Spanish and eventually a PhD based on her creative dissertation, Plainswoman: The First Hundred Years, *from which the two of the poems below are reprinted. The author of ten books of poetry and two of fiction, West was a professor of English and creative writing at New Mexico State University and editor of* Puerto del Sol, *noted for its translations of contemporary Spanish, Latin American, and Caribbean poetry.* Tourists of the Revolution *was published in 2015 by Stephen F. Austin State University Press, and her selected poems,* The Red Book, *are forthcoming in 2017 from Stephen F. Austin State University Press.*

For a Long Winter*

I've always changed the fruit to store it,
boiling strawberries into furious jam,
flinging yeast over cling peaches
to bubble into wine, testing
the way of preservation.

Fruit moves too fast
from ripe to rotten. Dried pliable
in sun and air, it shrinks
leathery and wrinkled
but true as any Red Delicious on the branch.

Cupboards read like a museum:
Marmalade, Chutney,
North Orchard Pears.
The colors jell
in a year's worth of hoarded glass,
soft, deep colors of a healing wound.

Stir, turn,
holding what we love. Now

---

* R. F. McEwen writes, "I taught Kathleene West's work for years in my creative writing classes. I pick the poem that my students continually identified as their favorite. It turns a mundane task, canning fruit, into a memorable and, in some instances, profoundly artistic activity."

the compote melds its winter flavors.
Something settles on a shelf.

Plain Talk from the Platte River

You out there, flanked by mountain ranges,
the foothills dark with soaring fir and cedar,
speak of *plains*
as if you'd lose your breath
scaling the clods turned up by the plow,
as if the creeks had to be kicked
into the rivers, sluggish with boredom under a massive sky
that extends a sameness over miles
and miles of homely soil.

Why should water rush
to get away?
After rain, the Platte's as blue
as Crescent Lake, lingers
as the sun lingers on each glossy leaf
of the willow, the Russian olive,
waits for creeks and the ghosts of creeks
to join its leisurely stretch to the Missouri.
Lost Creek, Disappearing Creek,
Bone, Thin, Dry Creek
name the gullies, the cuts in the earth
where water might settle,
make the latent stream welcome as the child
named before birth.

Birth is a flood, extending generations of seed –
the plains ripple with their growing!
Full-headed wheat, the soft stems of soybeans,
grandly-tasseled corn outgrowing its furrow,
and milo, its leaves mimicking the distant flight of birds.
Fields swell with color!
The alfalfa waves crest and break in a spray of purple,
spattering the pastures with mauve.

And always, there is Sunflower
to preside over harvest.
Not corn knife, nor crop duster,
neither nickel-a-dozen bounty nor government spray
will keep away Sunflower.
Constant as the sun,
it nods its bloom across the plains.

This undulant beauty can take away
your breath and fill your eyes with tears.
If you are one to weep for love
or because of love
your tears will hold in the shallow corners of your eyes
as water seeks its own level
as the river whittles its banks
as the first rain clings to the windowpane
before it drops
and flattens into the earth.

Farm Wife*

A woman learns that it's more than wind and sun
that makes her weatherworn.
She remembers the man who said,
"You can't memorize the clouds."
His words sing in her mind,
a refrain from the song of her mother tongue,
a refrain more useful than prayer.
Over the pint-sized grave
the American preacher thumbed the Book
of Common Prayer. How common,
how expected, this ritual:

---

* Judith Sornberger writes, "So many of Kathleene West's poems speak eloquently on the theme of survival—one of the major themes, I believe, in Nebraska/Plains poetry. This poem deeply imagines a woman who's arrived there by wagon as she recalls her many losses along the way: 'abandoned hunks of furniture, / ancestors in heavy frames, / a child's frail bones . . .' Yet the farm wife's spirit has survived as her voice is raised 'not in grief, / but in praise of what she still protects.' I admire the stubborn celebration of this poem and the woman it depicts who savors life even after '[t]he dance and the occasion for lace are distant as the sea.'"

hunger no more, neither thirst any more
neither shall the sun light upon them
neither any heat

The sun beats down.
Clouds of dust and ash swirl, fill the trail behind
but she could wend her way back
even across the water.
Follow the sorrows, each conspicuous sacrifice,
connect them like dots:
abandoned hunks of furniture,
ancestors in heavy frames, a child's frail bones
blaze the trail with pain.

With each necessity forsaken, each small death,
she raises her voice not in grief,
but in praise of what she still protects –
the delicate china limbs of a figurine
caught, mid-whirl, in a dance
and deep in the trunk, beneath the flat layers
                                        of calico and linsey woolsey
the ripples of a petticoat, white and foaming as the sea.
The dance and the occasion for lace are distant as the sea.

Into the sun they walk, farmer and wife
pacing off the section.
The grasses rustle like crinoline!
Their beards twist into her stockings, small irritants
that cling as she breaks from the solemn counting
and hikes up her skirt to run,
run across the field!

This is the beginning – not of her life –
but of all stories hence.
Never will she tell her granddaughter,
"When I was young and beautiful in a village by the sea . . ."

Progression

You are the farmer's daughter,
corn-fed, apple-cheeked,
a local yokel from a jerkwater town
where tractors cruise the gut on Main Street
and Loretta keeps tabs from the five and dime.

You are the round little Swede,
snub-nosed, tongue-tied,
who rises at the crack of dawn
to milk the cows, slop the hogs
and cut across the corn to school.

You are the first to go to college
one hundred homesick miles away,
straw behind ear, manure on shoes,
and a coke date after the Kansas game
where Husky the Corncob yelled in your face.

You marry the hayseed in ROTC blue,
decided graduate school's not for you,
pack Sunbeam skillet and Bake-King tin
to honeymoon at the Holiday Inn
where Tom and Sharon put cornflakes in the bed
and undutiful thoughts come into your head.

You are not the first to divorce.
"Grandma did and *she* was good!"
but Grandmother left that city slicker,
let him go straight to the dogs with corn liquor
and settled down with an old-country man.

Your lovers are men who never remember
if you're Iowa-born or Dakota-bred
but they've all hit I-80 on the way to Frisco,
sent corny postcards from Bosselman's Cafe:
"God, but I miss you. God, but it's flat."

You are the ugly American
in blue jeans, t-shirts and mirror shades.
The dollar's strong, your accent's stronger,
cracking gum, munching popcorn, peanut butter, chocolate bars –
"Why *can't* the Europeans take us like we are?"

You are home again, home again, wiser of course.
"Fine," you practice, like a salesman's spiel.
The same old cornfield east of the house,
Mom and Dad on the stoop, with the usual joke.
"Always glad to see you come – always glad to see you go."

Stephen Behrendt

(1947–)

Stephen Behrendt was born in Marinette, Wisconsin, and took his PhD at the University of Wisconsin. He lives now in Nebraska, where he is George Holmes Distinguished Professor of English at the University of Nebraska–Lincoln. An international authority on British Romantic literature and culture, he is also a widely published poet. The most recent of his four collections is Refractions *(Shechem Press, 2014).*

Coyote

It's mid-afternoon, and a coyote, tan
as the dust of fallen aspen leaves,
is crossing the west pasture, eyeing me
as he runs, head curled back
over the right shoulder, trusting
the way is clear and straight ahead.

The dry brome strokes his sides,
his underbelly, his upcurved muzzle:
I watch it bend, wave and wake,
as his slender body parts the shafts.

Later this same coyote (we will know him
by his ragged ear) will cross the wrong field,
unwary, strike a fresh diagonal across
a neighbor's backlot filled with wildflowers,
with sage and mullein, spiderwort.

The first shot downs him, tearing
through left flank, soft ivory undercoat,
shatters the pelvis so he cannot stand.
Half-submerged amid the flowers,
he digs front claws into warm clay, draws
his body forward toward the rising moon.

The second shot fills the silence
of late September, expanding in the quiet

like thunder unanticipated; the second shot
shatters his skull, ruins the butter-colored fur,
the deep and glossy pupils behind grey lids
that will not rise again. The second shot
hangs in the air, brooding over the sharp
cry it cannot wholly silence.

Last Leaves

The spade-shaped leaves brown and crisp,
curling in the bean-field in September's drier heat
where the possums still pass at night
beneath the bare-faced moon, brushing the leaves
that crackle and break at their gentle pressure,
their humped shoulders, dragging tails.
Soon the harvest will happen, the stripped stalks fall,
chopped and shredded, swirling in the wind,
their summer's full load cupped in steel coffers.

In other fields the August mice, grown now, the voles,
the kittens that will catch them, devour them,
move beneath the rattling cornstalks' tawny spears
bent by wind and heat, exhausted, used up,
the dry ears they had sheathed and sheltered
gathered too, now, their close-packed proximity
heating the steel garners through the night.

Stevens Creek twists its narrow brown length
along the deep cuts beneath the still-green arches
of cottonwoods tilting from the undercut banks
pocked and rippled with the season's last fry,
the day-long lives floating on glassy, veined wings
or swirling slowly in shallow eddies,
caught by water and inexorable gravity.

Off to the south, borne on the sweeping wind
that dries the leaves, the grasses, the farmers' faces,
a thin twist of song tinged with autumn ochre

and the young widow's breathy, grieving tears
trails northward on the current from the burial plot,
the flag-draped coffin lowering slowly toward the earth
like the harvest moon growing larger, more pumpkin-hued,
the apple-heavy boughs pendant among clouds of midges,
petals of sunflower and autumn aster strewn from her hand,
the other holding by its finger-tips her straw-blonde daughter's
who weeps for sadness, for Daddy missing all this music,
all these flowers, who will not come back like flowers or crops,
nor rise in April with the iris whose varied lips and hues
speak of permanence, of seasons' circles and of summer song.

Susan Strayer Deal
(1948–2014)

Born in Lincoln, Susan L. Strayer graduated from Kearney State College (BA, 1973) and the University of Nebraska (MA, 1980), after which she taught high school and college English throughout Nebraska and the Midwest. Her verse collections included No Moving Parts *(1980) and* The Dark Is a Door *(1984). She received two Pushcart Prizes for her work, which appeared in numerous journals and anthologies under her married name, Susan Strayer Deal.*

Elegy

The boy who lost
his father on Friday
is an empty desk.
I imagine him
peeling back his grief
like a piece of fruit.
Finding the small seeds
stopped in the center
and they will be
hopelessly round.

I imagine him trying
to untangle his father
from the barbed wire
fence, where his father
is draped smelling
of shotgun shell.
The discharged gun
pointing into the sky.
Pheasants drifting over
the ruined body. The
deer hushed and
standing still.

I imagine him trying
to push back the eyes

of his father that are
cloudlike and rising
out of the body, into
the sky. I imagine
him trying to tie back
the loose tongue that is
dangling now between
truth and fiction and
the heart that has
dropped into stone and
the hands that will
not lead nor follow.

I imagine him trying
to remember his father
who is turning to seed
and to grasses, turning
into sap and branches quickly,
which he can not catch nor
handle inside his fumbling hands.

Distant Cousins*

At the end, I want to walk
up and over the next hill
to come down where they are
arranging themselves for
this last picture. Come
down and see how they have
pulled the upright piano
out of the soddy and every
chair. I want to find one
chair positioned to the side,
inviting me.

---

* Ted Kooser writes, "The late Susan Strayer wrote so many deeply moving poems that I find it hard to select a favorite. We know what sod house life was like from the Solomon Butcher photographs, and this poem uses not light but words to follow in that tradition. My favorite moment is 'I want to find one / chair positioned to the side, / inviting me.'"

Though they must sense me
coming, just out of their reach,
beyond their vision, a fifth or
sixth cousin, they look so tense
and so intent on showing a decent
posture to the world. As if they
didn't know what would come of
this or were afraid whose future
hands they would fall into.

I want to walk down and release
them into laughter. Send them back
off stage to where they best perform.
Him, not yet gnawed to death by wind,
back to the black fields plowing.
And her still undespairing to the
elderberries flooding the next canyon.
And I am here now, my hands on the
door of the picture, so that they
can, at last, let themselves go.

Kathleen Cain

(1948–)

Kathleen Cain is a fourth-generation Nebraskan. A 1970 UNL graduate, she moved to Colorado in 1972. She's maintained strong ties to Nebraska through family, friends, and literature. Her poetry appears in Late Bloomers *(1986) and has been widely published in anthologies and literary magazines. Her nonfiction book,* The Cottonwood Tree: An American Champion *(2007), was included in the Nebraska 150 Books list by the Nebraska Literary Heritage Association.*

1936

My father says it was bad management
on the part of the hired hand that lost the farm
but my grandfather blamed the drought
that he called *drouth*
and wrote to me about the hundred acres
of corn he planted
that didn't raise a sprout
and how the dust piled up against the door
like snow
and how they dipped the sheets
in water (before the well dried up)
and spread them over the babies' beds
and how my grandmother swept the floor
and swept the floor
and would not quit
even when he told her it was no use.

And then, he said, the cream checks were small
with the cattle bought off at what
someone called a bargain: twenty dollars each.
And my uncle Denny says how can anyone
expect *him* to remember the farm,
though they all do, that he was only three.

Then my father remembers them talking
in whispers about dinner.

If they came home with coffee
there was no sugar. Or no shoes.
If they could they drove to town.
It was hard to see in the dust
and the wind wouldn't stop.
And when my aunt Jeanne came to visit
last summer, she asked why the crops
weren't brown. She wanted to visit the graves
if she could bear it. And she was glad
the old house was torn down.

Sunset Clouds Rewrite History Outside Lincoln, Nebraska

for John V

Crazy Horse
rides north again,
this time
into shallow hills
where no one
will find him.

Dark barrels
of long rifles
take aim,
then dissipate.
Too late.
He's gone.

A salmon
swims down-
stream, searching
for its lost
river, though
not before
flames take
its bones
back to ash.

And if the sky
could utter
one single note
of praisesong
before dark,
it would
surely be
the first
pure sound
of fire
burning
out of
this ruby-
throated
silence.

Twyla M. Hansen
(1949–)

Twyla Hansen is Nebraska's State Poet (2013–2018) and co-directs the website Poetry from the Plains: A Nebraska Perspective. *Her new book is* Rock • Tree • Bird *(Backwaters, 2017). Two of her previous books won Nebraska Book Awards. Her writing is published in* Midwest Quarterly, Nebraska Life, Organization & Environment, Prairie Fire, Prairie Schooner, South Dakota Review, National Treasures of the Great Plains: An Ecological Perspective, Encyclopedia of the Great Plains, *the* Poetry Out Loud *anthology, and many others. Born in Omaha, she was raised on her Danish grandparents' farm in Burt County.*

We Are on Nine-Mile Prairie When

the news reaches us of twin towers and collapse,
walking with fourth-graders through tall grass,
our guide uttering bluestem and goldenrod, mammal
and snake, this early report not yet registering,

the sun high, burning. Standing on the unplowed,
the whole, no broken sod or surreal debris, only silence,
learning pollination and forb, coyote and mouse,
deer and split-hoof adaptation. This unspoiled place

a split screen – reels replaying later – spider and insect,
growth points above or below, roots with tentacles deeper
than imagination. How do we comprehend fanatics? Out here
we speak French – *prairie:* treeless meadow, evolving

through the millennia. Plant, animal, weather intertwined,
on each other dependent. The first people and fire, following
the source. Fourth grade, when school grows more complex,
when the curriculum includes heritage. How do we define

fear, the future, the dead? The blameless children, rabbits,
bolt from predators, crouch in grass. Nowhere to run, nowhere
to hide, no superman to reverse the earth's rotation, start
this day over. Wings in the air, the claws of terror. We pause

on thatch in the brief quiet, breathe unsullied air. While
winds blow our way, we search for words, phrases,
language that is truly alive. Are we safe on this, our only,
planet? Each child becoming the smallest prey.

9–11–01

After a Rain

After a rain I yank weeds in the flowerbed – crabgrass and foxtail,
the usual suspects – and because moisture is abundant, seedlings

of maple and ash, my own private forest, which undeniably multiplies
beneath the windbreak I planted years ago, where thanks to birds,
scores of young cedar, mulberry, wild cherry now tangle. For now

I concentrate on these out of place plants that arrived by airwaves
last season, graceful, on their single- and double-winged samaras.

As a child, I welcomed those helicopters, gathered them
and climbed to the height of the windmill to send a bucketful twirling
toward the gravel farm yard, my own private landing strip.

And Father recalling the Dirty Thirties, years when heat and drought
ganged up, searing young crops in fields, turning them white overnight.

Today, I count blessings: cool air, a rainbow of blooms, damp earth.
Even rain gutters unattended sprout things, leafy and green. Would
father grin at my yard, its overly dense and grandiose scheme?

Birds at the feeder make a joyful noise. I stand up, light-headed, giddy.
If I spread my arms, I could more or less abandon myself to the wind.

August 12 in the Nebraska Sand Hills Watching the Perseids Meteor Shower

In the middle of rolling grasslands, away from lights,
a moonless night untethers its wild polka-dots,
the formations we can name competing for attention
in a twinkling and crowded sky-bowl.

Out from the corners, our eyes detect a maverick meteor,
a transient streak, and lying back toward midnight
on the heft of car hood, all conversation blunted,
we are at once unnerved and somehow restored.

Out here, a furrow of spring-fed river threads
through ranches in the tens of thousands of acres.
Like cattle, we are powerless, by instinct can see
why early people trembled and deliberated the heavens.

Off in the distance those cattle make themselves known,
a bird song moves singular across the horizon.
Not yet 2:00, and bits of comet dust, the Perseids,
startle and skim the atmosphere like skipping stones.

In the leaden dark, we are utterly alone. As I rub the ridges
on the back of your hand, our love for all things warm
and pulsing crescendos toward dawn: this timeless awe,
your breath floating with mine upward into the stars.

Sandhill Cranes

We watch them feed in fields near the river,
stabbing at stubble with their dagger-beaks,
and overhead at dusk, flying back in loose drifts,

their guttural trills that can be heard for a mile,
the slow flap-wings, their ritual stilt-dances,
tall feathered bodies gathering and re-gathering –

cranes revered by cultures across the world,
native peoples who imitated their moves,
their hieroglyphs found in ancient temples –

this raucous tribe that speaks of survival,
among the oldest species on the planet,
success on sandbars in a narrow channel,

some half-million sandhills – named for the
grassed dunes that top an aquifer, potholes
and lakes and wetlands on the central flyway –

these living relicts unchanged in their migration
from Texas to Canada on a half-way stopover
for millions of years on the diminishing Platte.

Greg Kosmicki

(1949–)

Greg Kosmicki was born in Alliance, Nebraska, at Saint Joseph's Hospital, which was torn down sometime before the turn of the century. He grew up on a wheat farm three miles north of where Carhenge would later be erected, a mile and a half from where his mother had lived in the sod house where she was born. His mother and father met at a dance in a town on the Niobrara that no longer exists. He has published five books and seven chapbooks of poems and founded the Backwaters Press in Omaha. He and his wife, Debbie, are parents of three, grandparents of two.

My Flag*

It is after dinner and I go to shake
the crumbs from the tablecloth.
They fall down onto the porch steps

for the crickets and the mice and ants.
We live in a great country
there is enough for all.

The tablecloth unfurls lightly on the held breath
of the still Fall night air
and it seems to me to be like a flag

with the blue stripe all around the border
and the blue stripe enclosing the field at center
a field which encloses some flowers

but could not hold in even all the flowers
since some of them have escaped
and drifted, as on water or a breeze

toward the bright blue border.
It is the flag of the friendly country
where even the vermin have enough to eat

---

* Marge Saiser writes, "This poem communicates so well, using ordinary things in such a remarkable way that a tablecloth can become a symbol of love for all human beings."

and I'm waving it from my porch for you
I want you to come and join me
and my family, I want you to sit

at my table and have bread and lasagna with us
so we can talk about the war and taxes
I want you to help me shake crumbs on the porch

I want to wash it and iron it and fold it safely
to place it gently and with respect in the drawer
for our next dinner when we will not have

marched under any other flag
for I know you could not be a traitor to me
we will all be so insanely happy

we had not yet had to die for any cause
I want you to spill your wine
I want you to get bread crumbs on my flag.

Deodorant

Audrey comes down the stairs crying,
this time it's antiperspirant
in the left eye
she can't believe how stupid she is.

We put her under the tap
but the chemicals
she wears to hide the fact
she is actually human
made of sweat, grease, oils, dirt,
will not flush out so easily.
These ones are guaranteed, I think
for fourteen hours to keep
from letting anyone see
that inside this skin
she lives in like an advertisement
for a hundred different products

is only a little girl,
my fourteen-year-old daughter
who can't understand how she could do this feat –

The Amazing Audrey will now place
antiperspirant directly into her open eye

anymore than she is able to understand, she says
how that morning last winter
it came to pass that I must rescue her
like a person in space tangled
in her life support system,
from her hot comb, by cutting
away her hair, her golden hair
like tiny strands of rope
furiously knotted to the core of absurdity,
so that when each one eventually was scissored in two
she was able to drift back to me
happy again, embarrassed, and free.

We sluice her eye
but the antiperspirant is stronger
than the universal solvent
so we settle finally upon Visine.
We sit together on the steps,
she in her golden almost-a-woman's body,
I in my old man fat,
and I see the two lines that run across her forehead
like the ones in mine from laughing and crying,
see how much even in our faces we are tied together,
and put the drops into that fragile place
from where she looks out at me,
where light comes into her body.

Sitting in a Concrete Parking Garage

at lunchtime to eat some raviolis out of a plastic container
that one time held sour cream
or what passes nowdays for sour cream,

I see the grain of the plywood the workers
used to make their forms
when they poured this thick wall in front of me,

and I see on the post that supports the ceiling
some numbers written in pencil
probably too by one of the workers

when they constructed this garage
and the numbers written on the post
make me think of my father

as numbers penciled in on any piece of construction always do,
for as a child I watched him work, hanging sheet rock
nailing studs together, framing, building

something permanent, as I have never bothered
to learn how to do, and I remember the magic,
that he could take out his pencil and make numbers

that would eventually be boarded in and not seen forever,
and the power, too, that went with being one
with permission to write things down on places

where it was forbidden for me to do so.
Now, forty years later, I am sitting in a car in a concrete garage
close, I hope, to the middle of my life

while he nears the end of his
with one thing after the other going wrong
like an old house you work on

but never can finish, because when you get one thing done
two more things fall apart. But when they do
and it's your body, you can't open it up

tear off an old set of lungs like cupboards
from the kitchen wall, knock the skin open like plaster,
find the secret calculations someone left there

that explain how they reached this exact configuration,
how many yards of arteries, the exact spacing of the bones like studs,
the number of feet of capillaries, calculated by hand

with a rectangular yellow pencil,
when your body was new construction,
all the work done on it, still known by heart.

Marcia Southwick

(1949–)

Marcia Southwick was a tenured professor at the University of Nebraska–Lincoln and now lives in New Mexico. She has written three books: The Night Won't Save Anyone *(University of Georgia Press),* Why the River Disappears *(Carnegie Mellon University Press), and* A Saturday Night at the Flying Dog, *winner of the Field Poetry Prize (Oberlin University Press). She currently works on legislation concerning the rights of elders and others trapped in court-appointed guardianships and runs a Facebook page with 150,000 followers called Boomers Against Elder Abuse.*

Small Difficulties

Is there any difference between what I am thinking
and the falling snow?
The snow is covering what I will soon forget:
the dry wheatfields, the pale leaves scattered everywhere
like small mistakes,
and the red house on the hill
where the neighbors sleep too soundly, like lovers
who haven't yet considered each other's faults.
To the snow, my footprints are small difficulties
to be taken care of later,
my breath and the cold air are a contradiction
of terms, and these words are like bird cries
that clutter the air for a moment, then die.
If it's true that I exist
in the shadow of my doubts, that have appeared, like bad weather,
out of nowhere,
then this would explain why I feel like timber
about to be cut down.
It would explain why there is something not quite right
about the ice on the pond,
which seems to give off a feeling of good intentions
even though it is dangerously thin,
and it would explain why the light of the moon outwits me
when it fails to enter my bedroom window
on the nights I wake from sleep and need to know

exactly where I am.
It would also explain why tomorrow, as it comes closer,
seems to have the look
of already having been lived in.
And yet the sun still bothers to rise and set
over the dark barns and fields of disinterested cattle,
and the wind still bothers to touch the abandoned silos
as if to reassure them that they are still there.
So perhaps it's true that not all is lost.
The snow as it falls is repeating itself.
Over and over, it repeats what it is.

The Ruins*

I'd bury my face in my hands but
somebody has to do it,
set the records straight: the combs were hers, the razors were his,
and the naked wax doll with the head missing
was mine. I'll step away from the ruins into the sunset.
I'll take a match to the whole thing,
I'll throw it away, the paper.

In the old days, the sun
was stronger,
so full of ambition that it saw through pockets
and blindfolds. No more.
They've taken away birds, they've taken down rafters.
I'm on display, and the sun watches me –
that's wrong,
it's completely self-possessed.

What if I've become one with the rubble?
Do I matter less than splinters of glass?

---

* Jim Cihlar writes, "I remember hearing Marcia read this poem in the John H. Ames Series in the Heritage Room at the Bennett Martin Public Library in Lincoln in 1992. The syntax of this poem sticks with me, as it mirrors the speaker's attempt to be logical about an illogical situation: assertion is followed by contradiction is followed by catalog, etc., but by the end we understand that meaning exists in metaphor."

Do I matter less than spaces where doors used to be?
A button I've lost turns up –
it's here in the ashes, and so are my old gloves.
Why do my hands cast shadows on broken white walls?
A last bird cries, making a wild guess.

Here, nothing is private:
The dirt, camouflaged by scorched grass,
shows through in spots like
bare skin on a dead horse's hide.
A few more leaves are absent today,
and everyone knows it.

Lenora Castillo

(1950–)

Lenora Castillo was born near Morrill, Nebraska. In 1996 she received a BA in English from the University of Nebraska–Lincoln and an MA from Iowa State University in 1998. Her poetry has appeared in several publications over the years, including the Nebraska Poets Calendar, Voces: Latina/Chicana Emerging Issues *(UC Davis),* Poets in the Gallery: American Nile *(St. Paul, Minn.), and in a cooperative book with printmaker Karen Kunc called* On This Land.

La Nebraska

The promise of work brought my family north
crossing the never-ending Texas plain
in a tarp-covered truck.
Torn from a long tradition of family gatherings,
bodas, quinceañeras and christenings
we watched in silence
as the undulating heat made the miles of highway disappear.

My mother, feet swollen and pregnant
stood beside my father, four children pressed around her.
Other families exchanged words of encouragement
and made promesas to the saints for a safe, fast trip
but there was always another town,
a few more miles.

In Colorado,
long rows of barracks-like buildings welcomed us
as we stepped off the truck.
Questions of "who can work" quickly reduced our family to tally marks
on a clipboard: 4 workers, 2 babies.
Sleep eventually caught up with us as we inched our way
through food lines, blanket lines.

The first truck, bound for Montana, came and went,
its quota filled
leaving behind disappointed faces and talk of

the next one, the next one will be for us.
Children laughed and played, making friendships
that could last days
if they were lucky
hours if they weren't.

Two weeks went by, another truck arrived.
Single men, couples and families (my family) boarded,
filling a wish-list from farmers in a state called Nebraska.

Nebraska, 1950.
We arrived on a small farm in the middle of nowhere.
Here, the air was clear and fresh like the ice cold well-water
that quenched our thirst.
Scottsbluff Monument, a dark apparition rising from the flat prairie,
silently watched us through the cracks in our walls.

Nebraska,
a good place to work and raise children my parents decide
but the others packed their belongings,
afraid of snow and ice of winter and tornadoes
that fall out of the sky like thin, black snakes from a torn gunny sack.
We promised to carry on the traditions: family gatherings, bodas, quinceañeras,
and christenings.
No they said.
There are no barrios here, no corner drugstores.
No hay gente.
There is nothing but the wind that moans like the Llorona
looking for her children.

We watched in silence as they disappeared in the undulating heat.

Terese Svoboda
(1950–)

A 2013 Guggenheim Fellow, Terese Svoboda is the author of seven novels, seven books of poetry, a memoir, a book of translation from the Nuer, and a biography of the radical poet Lola Ridge. When the Next Big War Blows Down the Valley: Selected and New Poems, 1985–2015 *was published in 2015,* Professor Harriman's Steam Air-Ship *in 2016, and* Live Sacrifice*, a book of stories, in 2017. She was born in Ogallala, Nebraska.*

Sex and Class and Race

Books say parents
didn't mourn their children

in previous centuries, that
nose-wipes and infants

died as edelweiss on a granite face,
so much sex in excess.

But at the very least, the poor
had their need for labor.

Perhaps the rich left children
to wolves or footmen,

perhaps they saw a child
as a purse divided.

Perhaps.

But even their women ran
into the snow, not to return,

or cut something again and again
so it wouldn't mend.

Yet people do forget.
Even I forget,

blind in the dark passage,
bent as the Victorian foliage

that screens me from them,
so sepia-dirty in their sullen

photos they might be another race
if color is what it takes

to dodge such sorrow.

The Ranchhand's Daughter

I

Not even the Indians who worshiped land
could abide this barrenness. They shunned it,
left bears' bones at its spent perimeter.
Blasting the presidents' faces in made
for a helluva slide, tourists, exits
lined with arches framing Ozymandian
reaches. When herds die in these ravines, no one
notices until spring when snowmobiles
whine, flipping over the drifts, landing
upright. And if sometimes stories circulate
about big spreads and the ranchhand's daughter,
it's only the Badlands seeking substance.
With its goddess rising from a shell sunk
in the ooze of lost natural gas, with flames
obviously next, like scarves when the wind
whips up, which it always does, the land swims
against the sun, against the unending
anonymous roll of the hills, perfect
for the innocent goddess, the hulking
he-god, the forever-kneeling supplicant.

II

Junco, meadowlark, warbler, hawk burst up
out of the sagebrush like a backshuffled
card deck as she drove forward with nothing
for a road. She didn't know any better, the web
of interstate thinned forty miles beyond
their three sections and the county seldom
fixed washouts. Her Chevy pickup took drops
the way a horse would, solemn and picky.
Right where the Lazy Y creekbed lent view
to the gully, canyon really, the walls ran
red yellow blue green welts along the side.
Although beauty burst from her at eighteen,
she knew best the grimy eyeletted moon
hanging a foot out of the trash dump.
Her wheels shivvied rock, then she tried to turn,
a couple of steers looked up, bothered, and
the salt lick in the back shifted so far
her front wheels left the ground, turning over.
To that, the radio popped on, the steers
drummed off, and all the birds in a mile hid.

III

Blair wasn't much of a nurse. He cranked up
the heat, served spaghetti out of a can,
and killed flies. She didn't die. Doc Parks,
the vet, set the bones. He happened to see
the fire. *Keep ice on her. You got ice?* Blair
frowned *Yes*, and the ranch hand fetched it. *You should*
haul her out to the hospital despite
the trouble with her mother. Blair left the room.
Doc Parks put a vial on the old bureau.
Ernie – the hand was back – *These are for horses.*
Tell Blair to halve them before he feeds her.
And if she gets a fever, send for me.

She fevered. Blair took his car into town
and got drunk. She was in the talking sweats

when Ernie found her and made compresses
soaked in coffee. Didn't have no tea. After
he put out the feed, he sat by her bed
reading horoscopes from last week's paper.
Then, dreaming, there was her mother, alive,
sawhorse legs, double belly, cigarette
breath from smoking them up so fast she had
to go to town and going finally
out to the hospital cemetery
where for some reason a red cactus grew up
that never had to be watered. He woke.

IV

Once in a while Blair'll stop at the soddie.
The vetch is so high there you almost can't
get inside but you know when you're in it –
it's chilly and the wind stops. This last time
he could still hear the neighbor twenty miles
off in his spray plane. He shivered. The cold
made him feel in hell. Funny, being cold,
the window hole hot to the floor with light
poured on it. I'd like to start fresh, he thought
but that would be fresh like fish, eyes clouded,
gills stinking, a smell for something living
too far away. I'd like to start –
It isn't for nothing I have her come
to me. They say the drop of a donkey
and a mule is worthless. I say it goes
back to the mare. I want her mother, over
and over. All I have is need shaking
in my hands, a corner that I bite from,

backed into. Oh, wife. He spotted the fake bronze
plaque the Duchess County Historical
Society put up saying this was
Jesse James' hideout when he laid low
disguised as a woman. Blair always felt
embarrassed by it. Before she was gone,
his wife said, *You missed your time. You should*

have a real gun, fine boots, and luck at cards.
He punched the two-foot-thick wall but didn't
do much else. There's the mark, a clod short that side,
under the picture of the Virgin. Hey,
that's who it is. I'll be. The dark litho
fluttered. With one broad filthy finger he
smoothed it, then stood there in a daze, sensing
worship wouldn't matter, having little
to do with either him or his daughter.

V

Only a slight rolling, the sand bedspread
rumpled, the chenille tufts pockets of sage
so spicy burnt that the ash had a taste.
Only a slight rolling generally,
the gully full of skulls, the sky bending
over a big blue backache. She's mended,
the horizon so bright under her blind,
pulling it down was an escape. Only
on Sundays did they do no work and she hid.
Blair – why should she call him father? – stayed
waiting alone until he shouted for her.
She ran off to the trap room once, in amongst
the spiked metal that smelled of rust and blood.
But he came for her. The hired hand played pool
just yards away in his bunkhouse or sat
in his naugahyde recliner fixing
harness or polishing his pneumatic bow
and arrow. From his picture window
(the house being trailered from Ovid) lay
her car, still twisted. He would work on it,
but not Sundays he told her, he didn't like
being so close to the house then, though why
he never said, a dog's caution, maybe.

VI

Double eight ball over, sun in clover,
you're my lover or some such palaver

on the radio. The girl came running,
the screen door banging over and over,
running as best she could with one leg still
screwed up out to the trap room which was strange,
given how much she hated that skinning
business, then Blair, coming after, but
insistent, calling as if he really
really wanted to find her. Blair's wife
used to say, *Ernie, you're gonna get curtains*
if I have to use my old half slips. Of course
real long ago. He turned from the window.
On the arm of his recliner he'd found
the girl's name scratched in, just yesterday he'd
seen it, watching TV, the rest of him
sleeping. Colt-legged she was when he'd come,
grizzled from too long on a road crew. When
she turned sixteen, and her father refused
to pay money to bus her to high school,
he'd felt sorry. He'd found a coyote cub
and brought it in a box to her, leaving
it alongside the porch. But Blair found it,
slit its throat before she saw it. *Good work,*
Blair'd praised him, *Got to get at them young.*
Ernie'd nodded, took off the pelt, stuffed it
into a wall crack in his cold front room.

And she stumbled out sobbing.

VII

Mother, I lost the doll you once twisted
out of cornsilk for me. It was better
than Barbie. I still watch all the programs
you used to, and iron too. The sand cranes
still come in the spring, so like the flapping birds
you made from newspaper, and storks too. Storks.
I was nine when you died, no baby but
not yet grown. You didn't say much except
that TV told some real bad fairytales.
We were sad about you together, Mom,

then just I was sad. But you often teased
Ernie, Dad says it, so I must come out
of a line of this type lady who likes
it. I'm sorry but I don't though. I like
catkins on my cheeks better, or nothing.
Yesterday I couldn't come visit you
because he hadn't yet. I love the square
with your name written in so the warblers can
pick at the June bugs that stray over,
and all the wind hollering down the slope
to where there's a real road and a place for
signs. I'm glad you're in the hospital lot
even if Dad says it's for bad women.

VIII

Mallards dive into the bright green custard.
Frogs lay their eggs in it, so thick they hatch
airborne, and none escape the hungry ducks.
So few cows commence to drink from this spring
that the grass at its edges is a downy
green, a velveteen. She smoothes her hand
across it, expecting a stain. She's
never been here before, though she's driven
or walked far into her father's land. Slow
as a miracle asked for, the sun crops
a lone tree and the effort of the day
touches itself. She punches on the car
lights, holding the mirage before her like
Jell-O over an oven, or moments
of television, then she turns toward stars
high enough in the horizon that they're
not fake and, keeping far from the dead cow
with calf mostly eaten, she drives straight home.

IX

The horizon was what barred her. If she
put her hand up, she could grab it, if she
drove, there wasn't any way to get there.

School proved to be torture, a one-room-rule,
every kid as badassed as the bus that
brought them, and her, the farthest, five a.m.,
first stop, seven return, the last hour just
her and fat Mrs. Finstrom, the driver/
substitute who admired the cornsilk doll
she kept inside her jacket, who once gave her
a pair of pantyhose and then died of
insulin shock, or, some of the bad kids
said, of overeating. No one came home
with her to play – but this was normal, she
didn't miss what she'd never had. Her breasts
budded, her majority came, eased in
by classmates pointing to the brown skirt spot,
singing out *Apple butter, Apple butter.*

When she started to fatten she ate less.
She unbuttoned her jeans, held them on with
rope, wore her blouses loose. Ernie caught her
saddling up, her scrawny arms high, her blouse
parting. Even he, motherless, with no
sisters, and a bachelor, could see the foal
coming. *That's something,* he said. *Your dad know?*
She hid her eyes. *No? You got to tell him.*
He dragged her off the horse by her jean loops.
Who was it, he roared halfway to the house,
Leonard? A half-breed selling satellite
dishes had come twice because she liked to
look at the pictures: aborigines
in Australia, spacemen in construction,
the dish a sort of hollyhock. Her dad
was with a sick cow both times so Ernie,
well, he sat and looked at the pictures too,
the first time, then couldn't take the repeat.
She shook her head while he shook her, then cowered:
He knows.
                    He let go her arm.
                                        Pardon me.

X

For three months Ernie kicked silence around
like an old cow flop. He didn't move fast,
polished up his one bareback trophy and
the floor clean enough to eat on. She swelled
like a two-door with a calf in the back.
Counting backward, Ernie ascertained that
Leonard was clear out of the county that
time, and pitied her. Then in cold December,
the wind unforgiving, the cows bawling
in the feedlot, when changing the oil
in the pickup took forever, Ernie went
out to check on the cows. The heifers stood
on their heaped-up silage and, grape-eyed, stretched
their necks, bitterly ululant. Because
the cow-scratcher flapped loose from the barbed wire?
No, the trough under the windmill was why –
Blair face down in it like he was looking
to part his hair at the bottom, and an extension plugged
to the floodlights sizzling next to his head.
Ernie said, *You wash up first.* She had his shirt
on over her ripped-up nightie, and Blair
was nude. *I don't know nothing.* Ernie shook
himself, climbed the fence, let the cows loose.

XI

She delivered that day. Twisting his lips
the way he did when pulling calves, he watched.
The girl got wild and sobbing but didn't
beg for no one, not mother, and no man,
and cursed its sex as it delivered. *Let it*
strangle. But Ernie cut the cord and laid
the baby by her. *Now,* he said, *we need*
relief. He dialed up emergency, then
swept the house. She couldn't leave. She tried, trailing
afterbirth like a cat.

Sometimes they turn
themselves in, but Ernie? Really? Sheriff

Potts waived bail and even the unit loaned
from the capitol couldn't do much more
than fingerprint him again. Neither of them
had an alibi. Who could stand as witness –
coyotes, cruising the rock-flecked range? She nursed
the baby through the inquest and wasn't
allowed to testify. Innocence sucked
in the silence. Perplexed, the judge deemed it
an accident, a man combing his hair,
nude, in winter, and a loose wire. She cried
then, shuddering, waking the baby.

The tractors didn't go for much, the cows,
once found, sold better, the auction drew more
than two hundred. People circled the trap
room and said what a fine-looking bride she'd
made, and how the little girl looked just like
her grandpa. But when Ernie showed up months
later to say she'd left for Montana,
that shocked them. All he had was the baby
and this dirty picture of the Virgin.

XII

And the ranchhand's so-called daughter? She grew
no way you'd think, raggy like the blue sage
even cows skip, not a tire tread against
drawn clouds, no John Deere beloveds rusting
heavenward. And she didn't grow wings to
satisfy whatever roan episode
myths shut on. She hunted for her mother
in more fertile quarter acres, and less,

in corn rows and pine forests, in lakes called
Mirror or Half Dollar, then she romanced
a park ranger to let her rappel down
the brow of one of those presidents. You
didn't read about it? *Oh father*, she
yelled, hugging him, *I'm not afraid of falling.*

Sylph

The creation myth
thinned
to matted hair
and a running stream.

Point of fact:
slime is what makes
the psyllium coat, okra-
green caught/carried off.

And sunlessness so interior
sound goes lipless. *Sylph*, she says,
rises, green clinging, all god,
no -dess for once.

The glade-light practices,
a Klieg advancing
sylvan, a deer forelegged
in adoration,

not the opposite of animal,
the terror of prairie,
what you came from,
mind made.

Susan Aizenberg

(1951–)

Susan Aizenberg is the author of Quiet City *(BkMk, 2015),* Muse *(Crab Orchard/ SIUP, 2002), and* Peru in Take Three: 2/AGNI New Poets Series *(Graywolf 1997) and co-editor with Erin Belieu of* The Extraordinary Tide: New Poetry by American Women *(Columbia, 2001). Her awards include a Nebraska Book Award for Poetry, VCU's Levis Prize, a Nebraska Arts Council Distinguished Artist Award, the Nebraska Library Association Mari Sandoz Award, and a Glenna Luschei Prairie Schooner award. She is Professor of English (emerita) at Creighton University.*

Meeting the Angel

from "Three Poems for Judi"

Not as a bird with twelve black wings and an eye
and a tongue for each of us. (Someone dies
each time he blinks.) And not shrouded in celestial
light, a fair-haired castrato. Not as Samael,
angel of poison, his venomous sword quivering
above the parched, open mouths of the dying.
He did not come as Azrael, *whom God helps,*
bearing apples so sweet their fragrance kills
our fear of leaving this known world. What did we
know of death, of suffering? Each day for weeks
we drove the autumn highway to the clinic,
where the angel's rough map ablated J.'s skin
with the blue tattoos of radiology, black
dissolve of surgical stitches. And like, or unlike
God, he was always with us, among the lush,
ongoing trees, the small mercies of fresh
air and afternoon light leavening the cracked
glass, our hearts' stutter, as we reached the exit.

Georgic on Waking

At the hour when the last streetlight
dims, resuming its dull face,
and the sky pales into the arcing
blues or greys you recognize
as morning, swim up slowly, careful
diver, and release, as you rise,
whatever catch you've netted.
Loosen the silky seine of your dreams,
its freight of skittering, rapid-eye
fish with their now-bright, now-murky
scales, their quick-darting fins,
night's shape-shifting images of memory
and desire receding as you surface.
Lie still until each shadowed corner
and shrouded, somehow unfamiliar,
object inhabiting your room assumes
the known geometries of daylight.
If alone, depend upon whatever sounds
honeycomb your window: a racket
of birds turfing out to the rhythm
of boot heels scuffling gravel, far trucks
downshifting, their hundred clearing
throats; on the good musk escaping
your skin, tart scent of sweat and lemon.
If good fortune's left its elusive mark,
the small heat of a lover's breath
beside you, count yourself lucky.
Let him sleep, but move against him,
until each pulsing curve and sheltering
angle fits completely. Let him sleep,
as you rest your palm beneath
whatever warms him, the antenna
of your fingertips light above his signaling
heart. Then speak that language
you knew before you knew language,
before you had to learn day's difficult
vocabulary, that yammering patois.

Mornings

Before the train screamed him through tunnels
to his windowless office, the idiots
he had to "sir," my father needed a space
without us, so in a crack of light from the bathroom,
he dressed, held his shoes by two fingers,
and left us sleeping. That walk

to the diner, the last stars fading out,
the sky lightening from black to blue to white,
was his time. He walked in all weather,
let each season touch him all over,
lifted his face to rain and sun. He liked
to watch the old houses stir awake
and nod to the woman in her slippers on 27th,
smoking as she strolled her little mutt.
To step back, smooth as Fred Astaire,
from the paperboy's wild toss.

Milk bottles sweated on doorsteps,
sweet cream on top, and once, he lifted a quart
from its wire basket, drank it down
beneath our neighbor's winking porch light,
and left the empty on the stoop.

JV Brummels

(1951–)

JV Brummels was born to a ranching/farming family in northern Nebraska and educated at the University of Nebraska and Syracuse University. His sixth full-length collection, frontpew@paradise, *was published by SEA Press in 2016. His work has been recognized with an NEA Literature Fellowship, the Elkhorn Prize, and the Mildred Bennett Award. His* Book of Grass *was awarded the 2008 Nebraska Book Award for Poetry. A longtime professor at Wayne State College, he's also published short fiction and a novel.*

Grass Widow*

After a cool dry spring the sun
finds a notch in the ozone
and burns through a lens of humidity.
Every pickup fishtails at every gravel corner.
Every driver knows the days are endless
but this season of getting it all done finite.

We adjust, change to fit the weather
the way over time an open wound
becomes a washed-out trace of scar,
and by the time the dry south wind is high
in the heavy heads of the cottonwoods
and my lip has shed its sunburn scab
I'm maybe ready to tell the story
I've tried to say so many times.
Maybe I've got my lip back.

And maybe all I can do is shuffle
the pieces and hold each shard
up to hot sunlight, hoping
for some vibration of recognition,
some whispered part of the whole truth.

---

* Kelly Weber writes, "I first heard JV read this at a First Fridays event in Norfolk, Nebraska, and the poem continues to transfix me now as it did then. Its backward sweeping through time, with images of a frail woman trying to survive the hardships of life on the Great Plains, speaks to me as a woman inheriting a life of wide skies, art, and sanity's threshold amid so much wind."

A day this spring:
I drive south across two counties,
the wet-paint splatter of drizzle
on the four-lane enough to idle
the chemical rigs in miles of fields,
earth no longer turned, simply
sterilized for a new crop no one wants.

To a courthouse, monumental
above the fastfood arches
and cars lined up for coffee
and some egg and pigmeat sandwiches,
maybe some flash-fried potatoes.

Past deputies and metal detectors,
the new terrific security,
to stand beside this young mother
at her arraignment. Her men are gone,
the first to a new woman north of the river,
the next to the place junkies go in lieu of jail.

What's behind it all? Some handy
farm or household chemicals
distilled and needled to the blood.
I witness her sign away her children.

The hanging judge harangues.
The silent reporter keeps it all in shorthand.
The marshal clasps his hands behind his back.
This present carries the weight of the past
like a heavy pistol high on the hip.

Back years: in the day
of zero tolerance and just say no,
thank you, I hold this woman
a girl no bigger than a whisper
on my lap while hand joins hand
joins hand as the joint is passed
around the kitchen table.

Back years again: WPA workers
finish pouring the counted tons
of concrete of this courthouse,
paint the halls and offices,
scatter ashtrays and spittoons
around the courtroom
where they'll be handy
for snuffdippers like me.

And again: just a meeting of two rivers,
some plank shacks on a mud street,
prostitutes waving from spindly balconies,
grass waving from the treeless hills above.

And somewhere anchored on that green sea
a young mother waits at a table in a soddy,
dust sifting on the fine-haired heads
of her toddling children, for a husband
gone after gold or the herds, his distant death
by drowning or bad horse or lightning bolt
bad news the wind is whispering.

Nevertheless New West True Gospel

Imagine there's no heaven . . .

Simple man past pride
school-teacher poor
up and over from the plains
on the backside of the front range
where money ain't nothing
but derivatives and change
I watch through this Saturday
this brand-new town
slithering across the valley floor

Enough to make eagles cry
I'm slaking my thirst

and my first
   legal Rocky Mountain high
in the Dusty Boot brewpub
among pioneer families
of accountants
   in madras sports shirts
short pants and flipflops
their tired women
   hair rinsed to faded gingham
pacifying the teething babies
   cranky in their laps

What a fool I look –
circuit-rider black hat
feet scuffed in authentic dirt
square on my round ass
like a kid mowing the lawn
   in crash helmet and pads
solitary behind bistro glass
studying Founders Avenue
a wide-angle view of a town
glittering in the sun like bricks
   of plastic-wrapped bank notes

the oldest monumental stack –
Established 2006 –
fronted by a bronze plaque
partnering the names
of the three rich and lucky
   hard-rock sons of bitches
who prospected this mother lode
   out of high thin air

What a failure I am
not to have struck here first
to speak only the language
of one lonely tribe
   among this earth's citizens

I lift my stare past the marquee
of summer sci-fi blockbusters
and the manufactured Italian place
  for the long view –
concentric rings of houses
  like brightly painted circled wagons
At least no steeples scratch
at the peace of the peaks

My business here's simple as ever
the oldest of professions –
trading grass for flesh
  flesh for grass –
between scrabbling out some few truths
amid the graves of many others
  buried bodies along the back trail
my only rule
  to break at least one rule
Beyond that I don't know what to do
but wave over the tab
leave green currency among plastic cash

Outside three tense deputies
study the façade of my fresh smile
as if this late in geologic time
any of us could do
  a damn thing about it

Charles Fort
(1951–)

Born in New Britain, Connecticut, Charles Fort is Emeritus Distinguished Reynolds Chair at the University of Nebraska at Kearney. He is the author of We Did Not Fear the Father: New and Selected Poems *(Red Hen Press) and* The Town Clock Burning *(Carnegie-Mellon Press, Classic Contemporaries Series). "We Did Not Fear the Father" appeared in* The Best American Poetry 2000, *and "The Vagrant Hours" in* The Best American Poetry 2003. *A MacDowell Fellow, Fort is the founder of the Wendy Fort Foundation Theater of Fine Arts.*

We Did Not Fear the Father

We did not fear the father as the barber who stood
like a general in a white jacket with a green visor cap.
For six long days he held a straight razor like a sword
until his porcelain-chrome chariot became a down-home chair.
The crop-eared son learned to see how a workingman's
day job after the night shift filled the son's small pockets
with licorice, filled the offering plate, and paid for the keeper
who clipped our grape vines under his own pageant.

We did not fear the father as landlord in our three-story tenement
who took charge of four apartments and the attic dwellers.
We searched each corner of the dirt cellar for a fuse box
while he broke out plasterboard upstairs with a sledgehammer.
We peeled out paper from wire mesh and read the headline news
a century old before he lifted us like birds into our bunk beds.

We did not fear the father until he entered the tomb of noise
for his night job, shaping molten steel into ball bearings
as we stared into the barbed grate where he stood
before the furnace sending smoke into the trees.

Fear became the eight-hour echo and glow inside his skull,
the high-pitched metal scraping our ears as our provider
left the factory floor with oil and sawdust inside his mouth
and punched out as the fermented daylight burned his eyes.
We did not fear our father until he stooped in the dark.

The Vagrant Hours

September

The month of sonnets:
The long distance runners roamed the hills
recited their poems in the afternoon and kissed.
The poet-professor in corduroy cuffed pants
daydreamed of the evening flask of black whiskey
his night watch over the hourglass of metaphors.
The young men were cumbersome in their stalls.

October

The month of sestinas:
The charm of lovers against the burred ivy walls
held the riddle of sixes and coaxed the student's heart
to a blackboard of pentagrams and tarot flames in chalk.
The griot's basket of apples, chestnuts, and maple leaves
held back the screen door of their teacher's writing studio.
The young women were cumbersome in their shawls.

November

The month of villanelles:
The young poet nods off in the back of the classroom
and a wooden pointer curled the cowlick on his head.
He was made to stand before the assembly and sing.
With long shadows and wings of the runners on the hill
into November's end and the town clock's vagrant hour
he lowered his head and begged a rhyme scheme for love.

December

The month of elegies:
They held the widow's wreath and opulent arms of death
kissed the child's thumb that broke out of a wool mitten.
They waited under a rain of taps and six-gun salute
for the son to place his hand on his father's cheek
for the wry minister to rise from his narrow chair
and place the widow's glove and ring in the tomb.

January

The month of blank verse:
They say he tracked a wounded animal
drop for drop for three and a half damn weeks
broke its fat neck barehanded dead and stirred
right strong coffee until he heard noises.
The hot prairie wind howled a fancy tune.
He knew it was a way of knowing things.

February

The month of ballads and woe:
The traveler brings a small gift to her screen door
and he barely remembers the song she whispered
sixteen years before under the lilac-covered bridge.
Was that her low voice rising above the top of trees
or a meteor with its own articulation of the heavens
in the arc of falling embers that filled the brown field?

March

The month of pantoums:
She stood for hours in mud
for a handsome young man
who turned into a beer slug
not a fine bottle of wine.

For a handsome young man
who turned into a beer slug
not a fine bottle of wine
she stood for hours in mud.

April

The month of odes and affliction:
This was not the cruelest nor a tepid month Mr. Eliot
until a letter arrived out of nowhere from a best friend
the best damned drinking friend twenty-six years ago.
He wrote about old poems that spent his failing heart
who had very little time in the red-stained hourglass
how he was on a waiting list for love and a new heart.

May

The month of heroic couplets:
Let there be thunder in his heart again
let a church bell's echo dance in his pen!
Where he erred once let him live twice
as he lived once let him sing with light
Let his hands turn the hourglass
and the last sailboat raise its mast!

June

The month of pastorals:
The poet met Art Pierce cliff side at Ojo Caliente
his calligraphy on clay birds in mosaic and arsenic
sent by the god of letters to the underworld spring.
They lifted their chalices to the crippled and mortal
who swam the miracle waters for the unkind rebirth
who sought refuge in the ghost chamber of the earth

July

The month of stanzas:
This was the month of writer's block.

Nothing moved his fingers on the typewriter
until rain outside his studio in the burnt sky
formed a rainbow in the watchmaker's eyepiece.
What landed on his bad shoulder a poor white raven
found in his good hand a ruby from the baker's oven.

August

The month of *vers libre* in his bare hands:
The poet learned the rules of open form
in the black ink spread across the pages
one misspelled word in the spelling bee.
He studied the burial ground of images
how love was subtle and hidden in a line
how love was metered and love was rare.

Art Homer

(1951–)

Art Homer taught poetry and nonfiction writing at the University of Nebraska Omaha for thirty-three years, retiring in 2015. His most recent of five poetry collections is Blind Uncle Night *(WordTech Press, 2012). His nonfiction book,* The Drownt Boy: An Ozark Tale *(University of Missouri Press), was a finalist for the AWP Award. He gave the 2014 guest lecture at the John Clare Festival in Helpston, England, the sesquicentennial of the poet's death. Art and his wife, poet and fine-press printer Alison Wilson, live in rural Nebraska in a house they largely built themselves.*

Turkey Vultures

The majority of the Universe – some 70% – is composed of dark energy,
an equally mysterious quantity which exerts negative pressure.
– from "Team Finds 'Proof' of Dark Matter," BBC News Service

Given wind enough these big birds
go acrobat, six foot plus of wing,
negative space against the year's first
thunderheads southwest.
                                        Barrel roll,
stall turn, everything short of loop.
Migrate by maintaining stall against
prevailing wind, wait a week for sun
and bloat to cook your meat, and you'd
stand on one wing in the face of storms
that emit lightning and a galaxy of cloud
and homeowners, pulling their sheets
off lines, colliding with their own
trash and patio furniture, the pulverized
receipts of dead deals blown from offices
of seed salesmen, cabs of grain trucks.

Vultures must absorb light, draggled stars
parked on snags and fence posts till the dew
evaporates from wing and back, must launch
themselves into thick air while blackbirds

and kingbirds strafe their bald grey pates.
Safe in the updrafts, they maintain their
septic orbit over the bluffs. I watch them
for the good news: uplift.
                                        Let the field sparrows'
cries rebound, the bluebirds and the cardinals
rejoice. Gouts of empty space, the vultures wheel
above them, lenses through the false blue
to all that lies beyond. What does the dark
matter if they are not afraid? Clouds gather
themselves unto themselves until we cannot
read their intent or direction. Safe in wind,
they know that clinging to the earth
is the surest way to be pulled apart.

Five A.M., That Small Problem Again

The moon's a gutted trout awash in dark
current I can't reach. I should sleep.
How blind uncle night baits hooks is none
of my concern. Some fool stuck carp scales
in my eyelid. Now they flash like stars.
Where are coyotes that used to wail steep
arpeggios over the lake? Their words and song
were one quick boat. Look, you can see the sails.

But why should I let sleep wear out my eyes –
one ear to the ground, the other pressed
to air that won't stop galloping in my chest?
The heart canters back and forth from fence
of ribs to open range that always lies
the other side of darkness, dream and silence.

Grace Bauer

(1952–)

Grace Bauer's latest book, Nowhere All at Once*, received the Society of Midland Authors' Book of the Year Award for 2015. Previous books include* Retreats & Recognitions*,* Beholding Eye*, and* The Women at the Well*. A twentieth-anniversary reissue of* The Women at the Well *was published by SFASU Press in 2016, and a new collection,* Mean/Time*, is forthcoming from the University of New Mexico Press. She has taught in the Creative Writing Program at the University of Nebraska–Lincoln since 1994.*

Great Plains Prayer

Bless us, Oh Lord,
and this our Jell-O. Our corn,
our steaks and kolaches.
Our heat indexes. Our wind chills.
Our sunsets and horizons.
Our endless waves of grain and grass.
Our ancestors who started out
for the coast but stopped half-way.
Our nostalgia for their calico,
their sod, their old homesteads.
Our denial of the meth labs
that have taken their place.
Bless our perseverance.
Our unerring politeness.
Our red state politics
and our white, white bread.
Bless our dubious status
as *tornado alley,* as *flyover zone*
and bless all those who fly over,
as well as those of us who, out of
choice or necessity or inertia –
forgive us, we know not why or what
we've done – but, by God, stayed.

Note from the Imaginary Daughter

I have no daughter. I desire none.
– Weldon Kees

Mother always swore your plunge was faked
so you could vanish – unknown – into travel.
I waited for a postcard – some sign I could take
as proof she was right. Some thread I'd unravel
back to you – wherever you were. Mexico,
she guessed.
In pictures you look sad but kind.
Mother said you were brilliant but confused.
She said I might not like the man I'd find –
if I ever did.
She said you'd only used
her love for art; still she wished you'd let her go
along.
She kept the poems. The paintings, too.
And I composed myself a father who
filled my desire – a man too real to mourn.
Some nights I dream you dead. Some days, unborn.

Neil Harrison
(1952–)

Neil Harrison was born in Norfolk, Nebraska. He holds a bachelor's degree in English and biology (Chadron State College, 1984), a master's degree in English (UNL, 1989), and a master of fine arts in creative writing, fiction (Vermont College, 2001). His poetry collections are In a River of Wind *(Bridge Burner's, 2000),* Into the River Canyon at Dusk *(Lone Willow, 2005), and* Back in the Animal Kingdom *(Pinyon Publishing, 2011).*

Spring Burial in the Sandhills

After the service, the slow procession,
a multi-hued line of pickups and cars,
mini-vans and SUVs trailing west
from the church, then south into the hills.

At the gravesite, the pastor's words
sweep east on the April wind,
and the faint trilling of cranes drifts down.

A carnival helix of the great wild birds
spirals upward far to the west,
winged escort singing you
up from the season of planting and birth,
out of the cyclic skein of time, where
what we here consign to the earth
has already flowered.

This Bike Path Now Called the Cowboy Trail

Years ago it was the Cowboy Line,
a Chicago and Northwestern Railway branch
angling north and west out of Fremont
to the depot and switchyard here in Norfolk,
through the great roundhouse and on to O'Neill,
then Valentine, Chadron, and into Wyoming.

Station helper in Spencer at fifteen,
Dad stuck with the railroad for forty-three years,
less two, for the Great War and convalescence
from the mustard gas that killed his best friend.
Plainview, Neligh, Winnetoon,
Bassett, Fremont, clerk, cashier,
then agent in Norfolk, dead at fifty-eight.

Years later, Mom told how she rode the train
out to Valentine to see her sister
on my uncle's ranch southwest of Crookston,
and Dad, on his way to pick her up
made it only as far as Long Pine,
his train bogged down, unable to buck
those towering winter-of-'49 drifts.

When I was twelve and my brother fourteen,
we walked west along those tracks,
each of us hunting a right-of-way,
flushing and missing bird after bird,
cursing and laughing, devil-may-care,
as yet unaware of the stories rooted
in that long pair of rails between us.

Judith Sornberger

(1952–)

Judith Sornberger was born in Omaha. Her BA, MA, and PhD in English are all from the University of Nebraska–Lincoln. Sornberger is the editor of All My Grandmothers Could Sing: Poems by Nebraska Women *(Free Rein Press). She is the author of six poetry collections—the full-length* Open Heart *(Calyx Press) and five chapbooks. Her full-length poetry collection* Practicing the World without You *is forthcoming from CavanKerry Press. Sornberger's prose memoir—*The Accidental Pilgrim: Finding God and His Mother in Tuscany*—was published by Shanti Arts Publications in 2015.*

My Twin Sons Talk with Me about Survival

Robinson Crusoe, one son says,
washed up on his island
more dead than alive.
Each time he tells the story differently,
emphasizing once which animal he killed
to make his boots and another time
what foods he feasted on, but each telling
requires the phrase *more dead than alive,*
as though the struggle wasn't with the sea
or with the wilds, but in the man himself.

My other son talks of the Kalahari.
Stranded there without water or food,
he'd cut a cactus open, drink the juice.
His teacher says she'd kill
an animal and drink its blood.
He believes she would, and wants to know
if I'd do the same.
If it were the difference between life . . .
I start to say, but he stops me:
It's okay, Mom, it'll never happen.

Yet, regularly as a pulse, they ask me
to tell the story of their early births:
how no one expected them to live but I,

and even I more demanded than expected it.
The part they won't let me omit
is how I cried the first time
I stood beside their isolettes,
how I couldn't breathe watching
their chests puff up and deflate
like sails ragged in a storm.
I think they believe in the tears
of that story or in the stubbornness
more than they do in the blood
the doctor sent into their fevered night
with a cargo of oxygen and no message of hope.

Wal-Mart Orchid

I shouldn't shop there.
No one should.
We should walk the ghostly aisles
of the shops we let it trample in our town.
Sing elegies of the hardware store
whose owner would examine
a leaf shot through with brown spots
and curled toward early death
and tell you how to save
the flowering crabtree.
Take out his catalog
when you asked for a finch feeder,
show you many possibilities,
order the one you wanted,
all the while talking of Rachel Carson.

No one at Wal-Mart invokes Rachel Carson
or notices which birds are disappearing
or talks about the poison pulsing
through our soil and bloodstreams.
There are no prophets here at Wal-Mart.
But there's birdseed in aisle eleven,
so I go there, and on my way to check out,

I spy a special display in Seasonal:
orchids planted in redwood chips,
yellow and pink blossoms perching
on their stems like speckled birds.

It's February, months away from
the first tulip in my garden.
And the orchid's only eight bucks,
so it hardly matters if my ignorance
of orchids kills it. See,
that's what I mean about Wal-Mart,
the way it makes even someone
like me, who has read Rachel Carson,
behave as though anything in this world
is disposable as long as it is cheap enough.

So I bring home my Wal-Mart orchid
set it in a west window, which it seems to like
because its one bloom holds on and on
even though it looks like it could fly
off any second. And I'm enamored of it
and pretty pleased with myself, too,
for getting such a good deal.

Later, when I find the blossom lying
on its side, a fallen fledgling,
I cradle it in my palm
all the way to the garbage.
I leave the plant in the window,
keep it watered, just in case,
even though an orchid without blossoms
is no pretty sight, and I've already gotten
my eight bucks' worth.

Maybe it's inertia that keeps me
from tossing it. Or empathy
for anything clinging to its green.
Of course, I'd like to think
it is the latter. As I'd like to think
it has sprouted three new flowers

a year later, because, even without trying,
sometimes I do what's right,
because, although I've fallen,
I'm forgiven.

Laura Tohe

(1952–)

Laura Tohe is Diné. She holds a PhD in English from UNL. A librettist and an award-winning poet, she has written four books, including an oral history book on the remaining Navajo Code Talkers. Her commissioned libretto, Enemy Slayer: A Navajo Oratorio, *made its world premiere in 2008 and was performed by the Phoenix Symphony Orchestra. She is Professor with Distinction in Indigenous Literature at Arizona State University and is the current Navajo Nation Poet Laureate.*

The Platte*

She would be my daughter
                    the Moonshell River

tonight she has caught the full moon
and holds it inside the fluid motion
of her eyes dancing in a winter blue Nebraska night

the song she hums is this miracle singing inside me

Platte Tooh Nílínígíí

Shi yázhí nahalingo nílí
                    Moonshell River yinílyé

dii tł'éé' ooljéé' haníibą́ą́z joot'ą'
hanák'eeshto' bii' jootągo ajilzhish
haigo dootł'izh ná'dle tł'éégo Nebéskadi

sin yee hatałígíí shi yí' diits'a nizhónígo at'é

---

* Dr. Tohe writes, "I recalled reading somewhere that the Plains tribes once called the Platte River the Moonshell River because trappers brought seashells up this waterway to trade for skins and other valuables. . . . I decided that if the child I was carrying was female, Moonshell might make a good name for her" ("Restoring the Creative Voice through Landscape," *Nebraska Humanities* 1, no. 2 [1995]: 25).

Ron Block
(1955–)

Ron Block grew up in Gothenburg, Nebraska, where his family has lived since the 1870s. He is the author of Dismal River *(poetry) and* The Dirty Shame Hotel and Other Stories. *Among his awards, he has received a Distinguished Achievement Fellowship from the Nebraska Arts Council and a Fellowship in Fiction from the National Endowment for the Arts. Since 2003, he has lived in South Jersey where he teaches at Rowan University.*

Nebraska

Bad neighborhoods don't scare me nearly as much
as the middle of nowhere; the flatlands make me want
to grab at fences to keep from floating off.
Irradiated, the grass pulls out like hair
by handfuls. The ghosts of thistles roll about
in the afterlife of tumbleweeds,
a retarded prophesy of the drought last year,
until barbed wire catches them trying to escape.

A dizzy jaybird sings for the flat, flat land,
a sympathetic monotone. The highest spot
on earth, a fence post, loses balance, leans.
Even gripping to the steering wheel
doesn't offer much to hang on to. The crosswind
catches a canoe strapped upside down on the cab.
I'm traveling Nebraska on two wheels.
The only thing that keeps me from toppling over
is the thought, Where would I topple into
in the middle of nowhere? Would I fall,
like a body struggling to stay awake,
back into myself with a jerk?
Would I grow weightless as a body in despair?

The road erodes. Grass rises up to rub
the underbelly of Foster's truck until it submits,
and I grip the steering wheel with both hands
just to keep the pickup shivering in place.

Salvage

When my father went bankrupt, we tried to salvage
what we could, hat forms and the antique tools,
the ripsaws painted with the covered bridges
of a sentimental past our town has never known
with its Quonset huts and its temporary buildings.

All day I thought of my father weeping in
his hands that morning, under a reproduction
of an old man praying over bread and soup,
his hands dry and full of stiff veins, perhaps
in shame at what people in that town would say.

In the back of the business, he had a pile of scrap iron,
channel iron, pipe, car frames, I-beams –
and with his welding wand he'd fuse the junk
into something useful that few in town would buy:
Cattle gates, stanchions, crowding alleys, calf tables.

If you live in the city, perhaps you cannot imagine
what these objects are. But you can probably imagine
the player-piano. We wrapped it in a log chain cradle.
This was the last work I did for my father while
he was still in business on his own in that town.

For years I helped him irrigate corn, mow hay,
set siphon tubes, drain an interstate lake
into a sandy field, cultivate the land
with a lister and go-dig, dragging a spring-
tooth harrow through the fallow dirt.

Resilient, he went bankrupt and then built
another business, and I worked with him,
salvaging houses for wood, salvaging chicken wire
to bury in the concrete floors, salvaging drill stem
to sell to ranchers who'd build it into corals.

We used the offset printing sheets of the town's
only newspaper to panel the walls with a backward
story of the town, and we salvaged center pivot
irrigation pipe for the frame of the building,
and then he took his chapter seven.

Before the sheriff came to change the locks,
I climbed on the tractor, which trembled, lifting
the salvaged piano on hydraulic hoists into the air.
I hauled it home to hide it from his creditors,
and in that small town, our neighbors heard the potholes

setting loose a drone. They stepped out on their porches
to see a player-piano wrapped in chains and swinging
wildly from a tractor's payload. They nodded at me
and kept quiet. They didn't need an explanation.
They knew exactly what the story was.

John Brehm

(1955–)

John Brehm was born and raised in Lincoln, Nebraska. He holds degrees from the University of Nebraska and Cornell University. He is the author of Help Is On the Way *and* Sea of Faith *and associate editor of* The Oxford Book of American Poetry. *His poems have appeared in* Poetry, Southern Review, The Sun, Gulf Coast, The Writer's Almanac, The Norton Introduction to Literature, *and many other journals and anthologies. He lives in Portland, Oregon.*

Nebraska

After watching
Nebraska

a film shot
entirely

in black
& white

in my
home state

I told my
friend as

the credits
rolled

"You know,
they shot

that in
color, that's

just what
Nebraska

looks
like" and

he said
"Really?"

and I said
"Jesus, no,

man,"
secretly

happy he
considered it.

Valid Photo Identification Required

I don't understand myself, nor do I know myself, nor
can I explain or prove who I am to anyone else.
All I know is that I'm a man who let his out-of-
state Driver's License expire and who
does not have his original Social Security Card,
(issued at birth?) or a copy of said document,
to obtain which one must have an unexpired
Driver's License, which requires, of course, a valid
Social Security Card. I needed something to get me
on a plane at LaGuardia. I did have a Birth Certificate,
and when I slid it tentatively under the bullet-proof
Plexiglas window at the Brooklyn Social Security Office
and said "What about this?" to the unexpectedly
sympathetic and ontologically sophisticated young
Asian-American man scanning my application
for a replacement card, he looked at me and said:
"This doesn't help. This just proves you were born.
We need proof of your continued existence."
I threw up my hands and looked down at my body,
as if to say, Well, I'm standing here, aren't I?
I admit I have not done much with this life.

I have failed at love, let down my friends,
ignored my best instincts and given my worst ones
free play, but for better or worse I have continued
to exist. Because if I hadn't continued to exist
I wouldn't be contemplating all the joys and deep
satisfactions of non-existence, as I am right now.
I don't imagine the dead are required to show papers
at every river crossing, or that only those with valid
photo ID are allowed into the caldron, or the
harpsichord concert, as the case may be. Often I wake
at 3 a.m., I wanted to tell him, with the night terrors,
scrambled fears of death, which would be one
of the privileges conferred exclusively upon the living,
and often I wish I could forget myself completely,
forget the fragile, worried, rabbit-hearted self
that seems to run my life, forget the whole
nightmarish mess – I wouldn't have that
feeling if I hadn't continued to exist, would I?
It's true, I wanted to confess, I have no children
to mirror me into the future, and mostly I only
half-inhabit the poems I've written, a ghostly
uneasy absence floating just below the lines.
In fact, from the Buddhist perspective
I don't exist, but neither do you, nor any of this.
A luminous emptiness is all there is.
Instead I tell him I just want to visit my parents,
for Christmas, in Nebraska, for christsakes.
Which was no help.

At the Poetry Reading

I can't keep my eyes off the poet's
wife's legs – they're so much more
beautiful than anything he might
be saying, though I'm no longer
in a position really to judge,
having stopped listening some time ago.
He's from the Iowa Writers' Workshop
and can therefore get along fine
without my attention. He started in
reading poems about his childhood –
barns, corn snakes, grade school, flowers,
that sort of stuff – the loss of
innocence he keeps talking about
between poems, which I can relate to,
especially under these circumstances.
Now he's on to science, a poem
about hydrogen, I think, he's trying
to imagine himself turning into hydrogen.
Maybe he'll succeed. I'm imagining
myself sliding up his wife's fluid,
rhythmic, lusciously curved, blackstockinged
legs, imagining them arched
around my shoulders, wrapped around my back.
My God, why doesn't he write poems about her!
He will, no doubt, once she leaves him,
leaves him for another poet, perhaps,
the observant, uninnocent one, who knows
a poem when it sits down in a room with him.

Gene Fendt

(1955–)

Gene Fendt was born in Rockford, Illinois, and grew up in Fond du Lac, Wisconsin, a town about as big as Kearney, where he has been teaching philosophy for thirty years. Besides five books on philosophical topics and numerous articles, he has published poetry in a variety of journals and won several Nebraska Arts Council awards for poetry (2006, 2009) and one for playwriting (1999). Most recently he won the 2015 Princemere Poetry Prize and the 2015 Gemini Magazine Poetry Competition; the latter poem ("Water") was nominated for a Pushcart.

Magister verborum

> *You open the prophets and your eyes are able to see*
> *nothing but the letters. But what can the letters say?*
> – Nikos Kazantzakis

That bent glyph is a monk
of the world's oldest order;
they've gone barefoot from the beginning,
for all of the stones tell stories,

so even when gone blind,
as many of their order have ended,
they know where they are by feeling
and the rhythms sured by their feet.

You must take off your shoes to follow,
and never carry a weapon.
First you will be given
a pruning hook and dibble;

you'll be working outside for years,
till the tools move with the flick
of thought's finger: the sky
opens perfect and blue through the leaves,

without flutter or coo
from the still brooding dove,
and the new bulbs pressed under the grass
leave the egg undisturbed in the nest.

One morning you will find by your bed
a fine long horse-hair brush;
you will learn to direct it by breathing,
and, brushing the path on your knees,

one day a low door will open,
a bent glyph beckon you follow,
and in you will go and then listen:

Ancient as the page itself,
he'll lead you under the coppled lintel
to a whisper of vellum feet,
opening black letters to self-lit rooms

of gold and lapis lazuli, the floors
of polished opal, adularia,
tourmaline, each stone a swirling
act of some great or lesser history;

the susurrant feet are a voice,
the whispering voice takes your ear,
the moment of hearing, you see;
the murmur opens to vision:

in this small green stone young Shakespeare sits
in his mother's garden, musing on
a bud of brighter green;
                                                  and in this blue-white-
flecked with brown, the men of Athens set out
against the Persians on the boards that were
their homes but yesterday
to fight for a tomorrow in the stones
set after them row on row;

we read now that they won,
but in this swirling stone
their hearts are in their throats, you see how fine
the fissuring stonework etches each expression;

in this long speckled one, the well-trained reader finds
the magic unwritten ending to Bach's
great final fugue, interrupted by
his dying prayer, unfinished on his desk,
but here, the original he wished to copy –
if you train your ears, these stones promise,
you shall hear, and hearing, return,
as Ulysses,
a wine-dark stain in moonstone two rooms down,
stands, returned to Ithaca, to hear the Sirens
while Penelope waits in bed.

The instruments
of our science are too gross to enter here –
debate still rages if this central floor,
the smallest room –
its columned clerestory open to heaven
doming over gold and lapis tracery, whence,
some say, all light here emanates –
is diamond or the adamantine axle end
Plato's myth said the world turned on;

that all the rooms are floored so we are sure,
for none has yet been found that is merely dirt,
though some, more modern, need constant sweeping,
and, open as it is, many dry brown leaves blow in
that are but leaves, and dry; they start fires
well enough to warm our hands,
while the Vandals, wild with rumour
of a city built in gold, rail at the secret
whose entrance is everywhere, if you have the key.

Our study today does not allow we look
at the first course of the wall, black marble
polished to reflective brilliance below the opal

and the gold, the floor, in it, only a possibility
and only that when the rooms are lit, as now

– so he continues on,
but you are rooted there,
seeing how the gold filigrees
into the real stars,

how, in the gathering black,
the open latticework shapes
your familiar constellations,
begins, magnificently, to turn.

And the walls slowly grow dark,
the floor glows warmly and fades;
the voices are gone, the night breezes rise
and drift a leaf to your face.

Wait in the invisible silence,
stand still there and soon you will hear
ten thousand hushed parchment soles
murmuring over the stones.

Mark Sanders

(1955–)

Mark Sanders was born in Creighton, Nebraska, and raised on the eastern rim of the Sandhills at Ord. His most recent collections of poetry are Conditions of Grace: New and Selected Poems *and* Landscapes, with Horses. *Recently, to celebrate Sandhills Press's thirty years of publishing, he published* A Sandhills Reader: Thirty Years of Great Writing from the Great Plains. *He is chair and professor of English and creative writing at Stephen F. Austin State University in Nacogdoches, Texas, where he and his wife, Kimberly, also operate a small peach orchard and horse farm.*

Plain Sense

Required, as a necessity requires.
– Wallace Stevens, "The Plain Sense of Things"

Plain speech for a plain people:
weather-words gray as old lumber;
old sheds and old houses
sitting on the tilted legs of wind;

verbs the cranes dancing, the snow geese dangling,
something wild dashed
into wilder brush or wood, the slow steady plow
of an idea through black dirt, the blossom.

We drive the long, sleepy phrases, and
turn sharp on a country thought;
the gravel punctuates, the noun-heart steers.
A sentence like a pivot: the steel spans circle;

the cold spray a nourishment, a continued green.

❋

Two ways of looking at things:

Rain falling onto your face from a black sky.
Or, the head turned toward the ground,
the face blurred in the puddle where rain drops.

In the snow funnel, walking blindly through the white of it,
frost in the beard, sweet moist on cold lips.
Or, still: an iced pond, a silver slip of creek.

The mouse in the alfalfa, the hawk's black eye.
Or: the turn, the absolute fall.
The beak, the flesh, the stone talons.

The ground, too, like stone.
Or, the mud temptation.
Or, the porous dark, the quilted bed, the dormant seed.

❊

A man wears a sandstone face.
Call it character.
Call it erosion.
Deep cuts, gradual smoothing, permanence.

❊

Every which way the wind:
the cattle-clouds, the skiff-snakes, the gnat-dust;
the dead dressed in green robes swaying, breathing, amorous.

❊

Old men passed us bottles of home-brew and we drank.
The taste bitter, the spillage dripping from the spigots of our faces.
The bitterness we recall as sweet: it was cold and wet on a parched day.

Old women poured us coffee from granite-wear pots.
Bavarian china chipped or cracked: chapped lips against our lips.
The hot potion we sweetened, clouded with cream or sipped straight and black.
The house was a mood: damask, vinegar, alum, dust.

❊

The swallow is a question mark, the fence posts exclamations.
The elliptical miles, the emphatic cottonwoods.

❊

Today, the tasseled breasts of corn, the bearded milo.
The wheat ambles and jigs; the alfalfa swims nude in a blue-green pond.
How can you doubt the optimism of hail, tornado, drought?

⁂

A child toes the dust and sees creation.
Someone dead smiles in the cloud.
A child picks up a stone and skims the water top.
More pleasure in plunking it to the depths.

A child dismembers a grasshopper.
Later, he puts it back together to dismember it again.

⁂

The metaphor went around the property.
Meshed, electric, paneled, barbed.
It sectioned the place like a quilt.
It linked.

Cattle did not wander, calves bawled and sucked.
Pigs squealed and the feeders banged.
Horses ran or lulled about, nodding.

It made the garden secure.

The city folk who came out to sell us something
had to stop at the gate where a big dog stood, growling,
baring its teeth.

⁂

A young woman once sat in a pickup truck
high atop a country hill, the hot then cold wind
blowing through open windows, her hair streaming her face,
the black clouds on the night sky
defining blackness.

The music was what she loved: the wind-moan,
the sky-sigh heavy, the cloud heart-knock.
The truck waltzed on its tires.

And best, most best: the sharp light like nerve-something, *yes,*
and, *yes, yes*, the thunder.

⁂

A plain word is a simple tool.
A nut tightened on its bolt,
the pieces holding.

⁂

The bull snake crawling on the blacktop
is exact.

The vapor, a heat-thing that crawls and disappears,
is exact.

The meadowlark, perched on a fencepost,
singing, is exact.

And when it flies away, and yet you hear the song,
and feel the heat coil or fly about you,
this is exact, too.

⁂

It has to have a certain flatness,
like old folks talking on a porch swing
under the bright bulbs of stars,
the electric buzz of cicadas, a chain creaking.
Soft words like the long smoke of a good cigar.

It has to be an observable silence, each spoken stone
compelling,
a flint,
or the snarl of a black cloud-wall just before the point is made.

✲

Our eyes hold the almighty sky in callused hands.
Our ears sip deep the odorous blue.

✲

The swirl of leaves
is the rattle of brown bones down casket roads.
The swirl of geese and crane,
their bell-gongs,
is trinity: birth, covenant, everlasting.

✲

An old farmer danced a polka with a pump handle.
All the old and young cows cried as the music poured.

He switched partners, holding hands with a hay hook,
swinging bales, the dust kicking its heels.

All day like this: everything a tune, everything a dance.
Even as he slept, there was a rhythm to it.

✲

There must be a recognition of need,
and need is the plain sense of things near.

✲

Out here, water is the great wheel turning.
Listen to the gurgling gears of pond, creek, river.

Out here, we stand at the center of the great wheel,
and we are the ponds, the creeks, the rivers.

So long as there is water, the necessary machine runs.

✲

Were the weather any different,
it would not be ours.
Neither the land, how it lifts and falls
the way a finch dips
or the steep to which the hawk glides
or the depths to which it plunges.
The burdens, the joys, the loves, broken things:
they would not be ours if they were different.

Anything else and we should destroy the essential:
the gopher-intelligence, the ground muscle,
the harvest-soul.

What is here is ours.
What is here suffices.

On Horseback, Hell's Gate Canyon, October

for Kimberly

We ride past basalt columns, ascend
a cow face to top an outcropping
above the Snake and sit there, and watch.

Here is the topography of desire: a sky heavy
with grey smoke, the blue and ancient river,
unrequited; the rogue, stiff bunch

of thistle and sage, brown, curled coneflowers,
and across the stream the accumulated green.
All those oppositions that pull toward a center.

Like the pleated hills of the canyon, distance
pushes away, pushes past an irreparable edge.
Yet here we are, two longtime lovers on horseback,

relics to a belief, putting the pieces together
that creation could not. Constancy a thing
like a slow horse plodding along the veins

that bighorn and cattle cut through rock.
Trust like giving the horse his head
to feel his way over stony rubble,

perilous going, getting there.

The Cannas

Blooms like battle plumes over her head,
the pug pokes out her flat face from between big leaves,
waits to ambush her sister stomping heavily by.
The hidden one crouches, black inside the shadows
of sun-reaching flowers.
                                        A poet friend once warned:
you can't write poems about dogs – it's the death of poetry,
ask Browning or Arnold. But it's not about dogs so much
as cannas, red and orange, green-leafed and chocolate,
towers of a castle on fire,
                                        and less about cannas
than pathways coursed, as a boy, inside my father's corner patch,
my own sister, her heart diseased, months from death,
plodding toward the swing where she flew until she'd vomit.
My assault awaited her, summer cooler under the cannas' dark umbrella.
Leaping out at her, we'd scream delight, race a circle around the house
that left her breathless.
                                        She'd sit and I'd run for the both of us.
As perhaps I still do, these years later. Like a dog's tenacity,
locking jaws onto a rope or sock and pulling for all its worth.
The cannas swing on small winds, blooms like tongues
as much as flames, leaves hands and arms waving goodbye or hello,
any way you look at it, perennial.

Michael Catherwood

(1956–)

Michael Catherwood's books include Dare *(Backwaters, 2006),* If You Turned Around Quickly *(Main Street Rag, 2016), and* Projector *(SFA Press, 2017). He has worked as a truck driver, weed whacker, garbage man, teacher, tutor, and administrator. He has taught creative writing at the University of Arkansas, University of Nebraska Omaha, and at Creighton University. Born in Omaha, he lives there now with his wife, Cindy.*

Balloons Drinks at the Frontier Tavern

As the Florence Days parade marched
down Thirtieth, Balloons,
with his jaw half-gone and fleshy,
sat in the Frontier slugging
one Manhattan after another,
the clink of ice
announcing survival.

The bartender stared at his head.
The world of chemo, Balloons replied,
then twisted balloons
into helicopters and giraffes
while paraders marched their way
into the Frontier. Shriners double-parked
tiny Mustangs in the back alley,
and Mayor O'Neill bought Falstaff
for the regulars. Balloons
pulled Idaho Reds from his pockets,
stabbed them angry
with cocktail straws.
A tuber pin cushion, he said, pointing.
Kids found their way in . . .
Balloons was there, they heard.

In '54 I began
the Florence Days parade

under a canopy
of trees, started
from Miller Park, led the police cars . . .
I rained candy on those kids.
The parade was five blocks long
then.
        Dutch elm hadn't rotted the trees.

And he sat in the corner,
plucking quarters
from children's ears,
bending straws into stickmen,
squeaking balloons
                                        into halos.

Projector

The 59 Dodge is parked in the driveway
where its tail fins stab the air, mirrors
gray with gravel roads. Here our lives are,
jumpy and crooked against the stucco,
Dad's practice swing a slow shadow
that folds across a burned-out lawn.

Eight months pregnant, Mom springs
from the Ford Fairlane wagon embarrassed.
Close up: her bright red lipstick disappears
into the house.
                                There's the old garage
before it collapsed, its hinged doors
cockeyed and wide open. The stucco
is in chunks under the window
where a rusted push mower points
to the fence. The film cuts
to Aunt Ethyl in her mid-forties,
the palm of her hand dramatic
for the camera.

Now the picture pans
by the cherry tree then across
the same peonies that still
madly bloom each May.
Great-grandmother Yonkovich
squints and stares into noon light,
no smile, her arms folded,
her Easter hat spun in satin and glitter.
Then the film turns white and blinding.

Allison Adelle Hedge Coke

(1958–)

Allison Adelle Hedge Coke's books include The Year of the Rat; Dog Road Woman; Off-Season City Pipe; Blood Run; Sing Poetry from the Indigenous Americas; Effigies I & Effigies II; Rock, Ghost, Willow, Deer; Burn; *and* Streaming. *Awards include an American Book Award, a King–Chavez–Parks Award, NWCA Lifetime Achievement Award, and a 2016 Library of Congress Witter Bynner Fellowship. She directs the Literary Sandhill CraneFest in Nebraska and is currently Distinguished Professor of Creative Writing at the University of California, Riverside.*

Waiting for Light

for Ted

Click click click on maple plank –
says she's seen some sense of light –
This rise, we'll move like prairie wolves toward
whatever's open, whatever receives poor
attempts at living, mutt and me, we'll be
quicker than the clicker she should be
trained with, now nestled in pockets,
in coats not come in time,
not ready for cold. Still a sense of here
is where we wring fear from fellows
born to page, pealing peel now pulp,
once slash-sewn fodder, click tickling ivories
atop some far forgotten upright,
across a keyboard floor we move to.
Is it the last of us? What leads us
past the last window where
each of us finds light, dust? Whether it's coal
on cars, the 4:11, or voices sometimes pressed
to make the curve, make the State shine.
Shine on they say, and in this near light
embodying morning.
Coal heads east on the 4:11

sounding through sleepy streets
rumbling brick pavement, glass panes.
Time for tea, or coffee,
maybe Sumatran, or Rooibos,
something imported, stamped.
Tornado-like whirring winds up, down rails,
velocity unknown, little matter,

inside this wood-floored, plaster-walled room.
Where the dog and I lie
waiting for sunrise,
waiting for light.

Then

Black Blizzard – hundreds of thousands of years to create the topsoil. Red from Oklahoma, Texas grey, brown Nebraska. The animals sensed it coming before the people. Chickens went to the coop and stayed there. The animals ran unsensibly, unreasonably. Clouds of dust made human figures in the wind. Could be an hour, or minutes to arrive. People fastened wires to the house to follow back – you could be blown away – Visibility no more than a few feet. Massive dusters. Some for days – during school hours – ten years of this. Silt on everything. Families daily digging out. Every surface in the house coated. Dust in food before it could be eaten, still eaten, field dirt with the food. Covering windows and doors with cloth, sheets, paste – air thickened, dimmed. Cloth to face felt awful – suffocating – dust, pneumonia took children. Radiation dry heat transfer, Kansas mercury 121. Insects seeking moisture, shade, centipedes, had to shake out shoes, sheets. Swarms – grasshoppers, gophers, birds gone from the dust, nothing to eat them – Jackrabbits multiplying, badgers, coyotes gone. 10,000 took part in a rabbit drive. 35,000 jacks caught in a pen. They clubbed them to kill them, men killing them, rabbits screaming, while static electricity, from friction, took lives, sparked everywhere. Plain sand charged metal, blue flames, ball lightning, same safety wires lined to find houses – cars charged up with static, knocked people out, livestock ran in circles, lungs filled with dust – dead – only water 100 feet below, Sears & Roebuck sold windmill kits to fix up. Dad, ten. People ate tumbleweeds, then.

James Cihlar
(1961–)

James Cihlar was born in Omaha. He attended Omaha Central High, and he earned his PhD in English from the University of Nebraska–Lincoln. He is the author of the poetry books Rancho Nostalgia *and* Undoing, *and the chapbooks* A Conversation with My Imaginary Daughter *and* Metaphysical Bailout. *His writing has appeared in* American Poetry Review, Nimrod, Prairie Schooner, Threepenny Review, *and* Lambda Literary Review. *He lives in St. Paul, Minnesota.*

Retrospective

Midnight in the middle of summer,
too hot to sleep,
my mother pulled the bedroom curtain aside

to reveal what I thought
was always out there: a kaleidoscope of eyes,
giant moths filling the pane, no two alike,

a reverse glass painting in shades of brown,
each pair of wings a set of eyes,
hundreds of moths pressing themselves

against the glass
until no bare space was left,
their wings unblinking, looking in.

This happens when we close our eyes,
she said. They come looking for something
that's not here.

We don't have the words to describe,
so we can't do anything
but keep the curtain closed

and know they are there.
That's how she taught me about memory,
an eye above my head.

Beautiful Living

Constructing spaces. Two red chairs in a casino.
Two red chairs in a funeral parlor.

Two photos in a living room,
you at the door. These words fill up the apartment.

Once I lived somewhere –
blue floral wallpaper, sagging balcony –

that I so filled up with worry
I had to move out.

Constructing buildings.
I watched the Missouri flow

outside my Algebra window.
Blue and white and brown.

Preserving houses. My mother drove me
to my first aunt's house perched on a hill

behind the black angel,
to my second aunt's house

with a deck over the woods,
where she puzzled over cooking oils

and rearranged the copper Revere ware,
looking out the windows,

and to my third aunt's house,
where my grandmother stayed in the guest room

with a half bath in the split level.
These words measure the footage

between the dovetail wainscoting
and the ceiling.

These words build a way back
to what should have been.

Recline in the dark-eaved bedroom
and listen to the fan's roar.

You would give me
what I wanted.

Now we are ready to commence
our living.

Kwame Dawes
(1962–)

Kwame Dawes is the author of twenty books of poetry and numerous other books of fiction, criticism, and essays. His most recent collection, City of Bones: A Testament *(Northwestern) appeared in 2017 along with* Speak from Here to There, *a co-written collection of verse with Australian poet John Kinsella, and* A Bloom of Stones, *a trilingual anthology of Haitian poetry written after the earthquake, which he edited. He is Glenna Luschei Editor of* Prairie Schooner, *teaches at the University of Nebraska, directs the African Poetry Book Fund, and is artistic director of the Calabash International Literary Festival.*

Détente

after Fences, *by August Wilson*

Then one day you know you do not believe
your own threats; you know that the mystery
of your wisdom is a lie, and you feel
like a fool staring him down, telling
him he must do as you say; you know
he doesn't have to, you know he will call
your bluff. A horse will die dumb,
that a leather strap dangling loosely
on the fence will hold him at bay,
keep him from drifting away; but not
this boy, he never stopped pulling
at it, and now you stand there looking
at him and you both know you have
nothing left, short of killing him.
And even then, he will fight back,
his body will take a blow and reshape
itself for more. All you have is bluster,
words, and your two long arms;
all you have is the guilt he must feel.
This is your son; this man,
this scowling fool who hates

you like you have never known
hate, who is thinking, you know,
of stepping on your chest, stomping
you down, like you did your own
father who cried like a baby,
crawling to the shelter of the live
oak, spitting blood, pleading
for mercy; and in that moment
he broke something in you, killed
that last abiding myth, the fence
around you. You tell yourself
he must never feel alone like that,
abandoned like that; no son of yours
must think of the world as bleak
as you did that night, walking
east like you was looking for Africa,
leaving behind the homestead,
the bed, the order of things, alone
now. You stand here now
waiting to tell a lie, waiting
to build a fence around you,
waiting like all fathers should.

Kelly Madigan

(1962–)

Kelly Madigan is the author of The Edge of Known Things, *a poetry collection (Stephen F. Austin State University Press, 2013), and a how-to book entitled* Getting Sober: A Practical Guide to Making It Through the First 30 Days *(McGraw-Hill, 2008). She is a recipient of a National Endowment for the Arts Fellowship in creative writing and the Distinguished Artist Award in Literature from the Nebraska Arts Council.*

Reliquary

Always I am taking the wounded from the mouth of the hungry,
the wet fur of the leveret from the jaws of the hound.

Or I am the one with the sledgehammer, the poisoned steak
that I slip over the fence after every authority refused
to quarantine the beast. I have to protect my own,

                    but the world assigns too many to me,
says they are each my own, the lobsters in the tank
at the market, the sparrows in the neighbor's trap,
the massive tawniness at the edge of the field at dusk.

                    I love the world that wants to eat me,
and I crave to devour it, too – smear my face with butter and grease,
talk into the night about meals I've had.

                    I am the paralyzed rescuer,
watching the nest mown over, waving from the porch
as the men head off with their long guns. If I have been sent here
for some task, I have blundered, I have failed.
I couldn't find the trap door, the men with the proper authority.

Yet I rest my feet in the stream and it washes me anyway,
and birds make nests of ribbons in my eaves. I am sorry. I was ill
equipped. I can't even tell you I will do better.

But I will collect the bones, I will stand
at the roadside and say your names: *Porcupine, Mule Deer, Wildcat.*
I will take what lasts longest, the jawbone set with jewels,
let it bleach in the white heat.

I will say I knew you, that I found it by Salt Creek,
or in the Big Horns. I will show the architecture of your mouth
to children. I will let them run their fingertips, whorled with identity,
over the tops of your marvelous teeth.

Nebraska

This is a place for things that take time. Long histories
that need to be unrolled and laid out across oak library tables,
with a hardback book set on each corner to keep them pressed open.
Here, we understand that shadows fold their wings and settle down
in midday, tucked underfoot like a coyote den the unschooled never
notice. We can see a fire in the next county, the smoke a thundercloud
of blackbirds twirling for fall, grouping and regrouping themselves
as though to remember something already lost, washed out
and splayed in the wet clay of the creek bed. You can drive
an entire afternoon here and not see a person, but all the way
the meadowlarks will be opening the doors of their throats,
letting out music like milkweed seeds delivered downwind.
You might start counting those birds after awhile, picture them
as mile markers on the telephone wires, wondering if you've seen
the same one over and over again. We have more stars here, so many
that strangers think there is something wrong with our sky, that it's
fake or that Sioux women have beaded our night with constellations
not seen in Minneapolis or Memphis, fresh ones that we can give
names to as we lie on the hood of the car. We can call one *Mountain
Lion Reclaims Ancestral Home*, after the cougar who roamed up
a wooded thicket into Omaha this fall, ranging until the zoo director
shot him with a tranquilizer dart. Here we can keep naming star puzzles
until the threat of sunrise blues the black space above us.
This is a place for things that take time, the long stitching together
of soft spots in the heart, the wind across the Missouri River Valley
scooping loess into hills unlike any others on this continent,

seeds stored in the cellar of the prairie for a hundred years
patient for fire, unable to crack themselves open without it.
This is a place where disappointments deep as aquifer
can spill themselves out, fill up and empty again, as many times
as the wound requires. This is a place where a person can heal,
or choose not to heal. We have both kinds.

Amy Plettner

(1963–)

Born in Omaha, Amy Plettner is an outdoor educator on Nebraska's endangered tallgrass prairie. Her poetry has been published in a variety of anthologies and journals, most recently The Sow's Ear Poetry Review, burntdistrict, Rattle, Prairie Wind, *and* The Untidy Season. *Her first book of poetry,* Undoing Orion's Belt, *is the seventh of the Kloefkorn series published by WSC Press. She holds an MFA from the University of Nebraska MFA in Writing program.*

Letter to Paul in Prison

after Joe Wilkins

April is a deafening pitch of frogs,
the air loose, the creek skipping high and golden.
In a fit of darkness, coyotes take to the mown path,
and off the dirt road empty beer cans
give way to green along the ditches.
They say a common snipe nested here last May,
her soft eyes all they remember.
The prairie's scheduled for fire
to paint it clean and black.
Even the heads of big bluestem,
wind stripped by winter, await combustion.

I stay in a sixty-year-old ranch house,
three miles south of the Denton Daily Double.
My neighbors wave, drive pickups with front loaders,
invite me in come foaling time.
I ask them about the snakes, yellow-bellied racers,
who take over my basement, March and April,
when the nights still forage on frost
and afternoon sun plays to their awakening bodies.
I like to think about them mating below me:
casual, slow, slow twists, and their distinct smell
rising through the register vents. I dream a rainforest.

You can hear prairie chickens across the highway
a vibration not like breath, or hum, or wind in a keyhole,
but more like the sound of that boy we knew
who would rock himself for hours
under the slide at the city park.
The man who knows birds says you can tell
a western meadowlark from an eastern strictly by ear.
The pair of Canada geese horn in low over the pond,
and ducks vanish under the silk surface.
Do you remember that Wednesday?
We climbed Platte Center's water tower –
the village lights, stars scattered at our feet.
Two cans of beer in your sweatshirt pocket
and a runaway moon.

Church Bulletin

The singing has already started,
and I stand in the back. My family's heads
lined up in two pews near the front,
same pews for forty years.
It looks as though a small child
sits between my sister and her husband

but it's really just a canyon
stretching its massive void, and what a great thing
to be able to say, *you're working on the marriage,*
instead of just in it, stuck, like logs
jammed in the river.

My brother's wife is missing altogether.
She's socializing with the millionaires
who can give her more than God.
Sometimes the church is like a bar –

all that light as powerful in its clarity
as the darkness, and my sibling's hair
is now many shades of cloudy sky.

They've transformed into adults, parents,
survivors, divorcees, forgetting at times
how to play, and open, and feel.

The church says, for joys,
Lord in your love, and for tragedy, *Lord*
in your mercy. Dad is closest to the aisle,
a quick escape, and Mom is shorter,
smaller, so much smaller. I walk to the family pew
taking my place among what's easily broken.
Close enough now to see my parents hands
each with matching bruises on the thin skin
beneath the knuckles. How has this day come?

The pastor is into his sermon
beginning with a clip of *The Lion King,*
and I think of my daughter at four years old
standing on the arm of the couch
in our apartment on 16th and Washington
holding up her stuffed lion, Simba, to the sun,
the way Rafiki does in the movie, and I'm a single
unwed mother on welfare, the woman
my Dad likes to rage of, and I've been to the well,
and the river, and the pump, and know my baptism
has come, and I am fully a part of this.

Steve Langan
(1965–)

Steve Langan was born in Milwaukee and raised in Omaha. He received degrees from the University of Nebraska Omaha and the University of Iowa Writers' Workshop. Langan is the author of Freezing, Notes on Exile and Other Poems, Meet Me at the Happy Bar, *and* What It Looks Like, How It Flies. *He teaches at the University of Nebraska MFA in Writing program, and he is founder and director of the Seven Doctors Project.*

Prairie Poem with Lines from Emily Dickinson

The roughened patch, family room, windows,
nothing's broken on the bedside table.

Days on the plains, slick surface settling outward,
the skyline's attached, we're wearing our boots.

You're saying, "I'm wearing my sun hat,
I'm staring at the plows and tractors now,
I'm watching the widows walk
into the post office, I'm helping calves
take their first steps!"

– and sore must be
the storm that could abash the bird
that kept so many warm.

– Darling, the rodeo's coming, let's go
watch them do their rodeo stuff.
Let's watch them do their end of the earth stuff.

When we go into town, we can talk to
the vegetable sellers, refinishers, waiters,
the sandblasters and one-hand drivers.

Let's live here forever – this broken wavering
spell – but only if you promise to say,

"Only through the grace of one crazed
and simple plan" when someone asks,
"Did you really live there then?"

And say – "I was happy there, almost glad."

The Book Finally with All the Misery in It

The book finally with all the misery in it.
The epigraph's crossed out, so is the appendix;

so is the sentence with the chorus
from the song we played thirty times a day

in 1989. I'm already tired of this century.
Mothers, children, their forgetful children.

I can't keep them all straight. We walk
into the arboretum for solace and inspiration

but that's not it – that doesn't do it at all –
and the racetrack doesn't need me anymore.

The tavern where we pronounced ourselves
man and wife doesn't need us;

the corner where the jukebox sat,
with my hand up her blouse, is a bare table.

The book with all the words I've
neglected to say to the mothers and children,

including *misery* and *finally*. Or the book
with the mother and her child and they're happy

or at least smiling in the photo on the back
cover of the book finally of misery

I've been telling you to read and, when you
won't read this book, I read to you from it.

The book of the dainty and the dead.
First chapter, dainty. Final chapter, dead.

And in between, irascible thieves broke
into our apartment, which gave us a story

to tell to our group of friends,
all of whom then shared their stories

of misery finally at the going-away party.

Erin Belieu
(1967–)

Born and raised in Omaha, Erin Belieu is the author of four award-winning collections of poetry, founding editor of Hotel Amerika*, co-founder of VIDA: Women in the Literary Arts, and director of the Creative Writing Program at Florida State University. With Susan Aizenberg, she co-edited* The Extraordinary Tide *(2002), an anthology of American women's poetry. Her most recent collection,* Slant Six *(2014), was named a top ten book of the year by the* New York Times Book Review.

Plainsong

He lived in a sod house,
a formal nest of grass
that wove green thread
around his soul, a bed
of mud and cellulose.

And she was small. She
never grew; the empty
wind that blew and reared
had bent her to the plains she cared
so little for. But he,

he didn't seem to mind
her size, he'd found
a shape to love there;
and she was spare where
he was generous as sand, the kind

of man who drifted
like the yellow hills that lifted
their sloping shoulders to the bad
lands. For her his mud
heart tumbled like the tufted

weeds that wheel along the plains,
that sea of mammoth bones,

that state all made of sky –
they married in July.
Her thin bouquet of corn

flowers remains the brightest thing
he'd ever see. I have her ring
now, a silver band so little
it won't budge over the knuckle
on my pinky. How long

ago, a man gave his grass
soul to her in her brown dress –
and she was always stern,
too small, and learned
to keep inside a sod house.

My Field Guide

I've never bothered with the names of flowers,
though now I'd like this expertise to call
them out to you as we hike in.

But I would want their true names, not
the guide's all-classifying explanations:

for *yellow simple-shaped* or *odd-*
belled purple cluster, I'd rather plump-girl-
shaking-her-hair-out-in-the-shower,
and violet-prom-dress-circa-1960.

Or better yet, I'd have the words
that droning bee has just now written at
the throat of lakeside goldenrod. They must
be intimate – see how he calms between her?

His body, only evolution's hunt
for agitation, yet the way he gentles at
her feathered mouth. Let's call that . . . what?

Biology is obvious. Or choose
another name. No matter how you speak,
what language we might settle on,

the woodpecker won't stop her rhythmic knocking
inside the arms of tamarack,

and we've arrived at birds and bees again.
But nothing is as simple, is it?

Joy Castro
(1967–)

Born in Miami, Joy Castro is the author of the memoirs The Truth Book *and* Island of Bones*, the literary thrillers* Hell or High Water *and* Nearer Home*, and the short fiction collection* How Winter Began. *Editor of the anthology* Family Trouble: Memoirists on the Hazards and Rewards of Revealing Family*, she teaches at the University of Nebraska–Lincoln.*

Chicken Sandwich, Alone, Café

I'm sorry for the fowl,
crammed and fattening in their pens
until death do them part.

Yet how delicious.
The air cool, strangers
passing, warm food in my mouth.

I'm sorry what we had
went south.

I'm sorry for the foul
rag and bone
shop of my heart

and for the way
I took my waking slow

– sorry that for so long
I didn't know
I'd sacrifice such a pretty pen
to my one art.

A Vertical Climb

to eight thousand feet is what you requested,
your voice a crackle in the cold, black night.
Rime ice lined the wings, revising
the very shape of flight. Spearing
steeper, higher, faster,
you broke through
to cruise
while we watched disaster
on the ground.

So smooth, you flew.
No one in the quiet cabin
knew what you'd eluded, your craft
so frail, so light.

Daniel Simon

(1967–)

Born in Fremont and raised along the Platte, Daniel Simon is the editor in chief of World Literature Today *magazine at the University of Oklahoma, where he also teaches for the Department of English. A poet and translator, he is the author of the verse collections* Cast Off *(2015) and* After Reading Everything *(2016). His work has been reprinted in the anthologies* World English Poetry *(2015) and* Oklahoma Poems . . . and Their Poets *(2014) and nominated for the PEN Center USA, Independent Publisher (IPPY), Nebraska Book, and Oklahoma Book awards as well as the Pushcart and Forward prizes. He lives in Norman, Oklahoma, with his wife and three daughters.*

Cast Off

Along the Platte, you don't need a stout-keeled ship
to navigate the channel, just a flat-bottomed skiff
in midsummer or a johnboat in winter scraped across the ice

Or in May, just strip down to your underwear and wade across
– on legs white like fish bellies with clothes bundled above your head –
to root around the island on a quest for pallid sponge morels

In a canoe, you can shoot between the pilings under the trestle –
driven like javelins into the bedrock – if you avoid the whirlpools
and logjams that snare prows and drag idlers down to uncertain fate

Along the shoreline lies the treacherous deep channel, created by riprap
and ice melt, which roils like a thundercloud sailing over the plains –
mirrored vortices sidling west to east, mutable iridescence of shadow and light

Midstream, sands shift underfoot but resolution must prevail,
each step forward a precipitous balance between folly and caution,
harpoons of thought cast forward, grappling hooks in midair

Portrait in 2/4

Not the refinement of the waltz
but the boozy, blue-collar polka for me.

Pla Mor, Starlite, Peony Park, Sokol Hall –
those Nebraska polka halls staged
pageants of folk exuberance,
oom-pah tubas and accordion flourishes
as men with farmer tans and shiny pates
swept stout women with doughy arms
in looping circles 'round wooden dance floors.

With beer and sausages, kolaches and coffee,
such Saturday-night escapes provided
a whirl of diversion against the flat plains
rising up into knolls, the hard life beaten back
beyond the edge of the parking lot.

                                                  Inside, the dancers
cast nimble shadows on the windows,
all while the 2/4 rhythm spilled over the edges
of the four-cornered hall, the music always flaring.

Matt Mason

(1968–)

Matt Mason has earned a Pushcart Prize and two Nebraska Book Awards; was a finalist for Nebraska State Poet; organized poetry programming with the State Department in Nepal, Romania, Botswana, and Belarus; and has over two hundred publications. His books include The Baby That Ate Cincinnati *and* Things We Don't Know We Don't Know. *Born in Omaha, Matt lives there with his wife, the poet Sarah McKinstry-Brown, and daughters Sophia and Lucia.*

Notes for My Daughter Against Chasing Storms

Tornadoes swing through like a kid
playing hopscotch, rip one house to splinters
and leave the neighbors unmussed,
up and down, here and there,
they flatten churches on Easter Sunday,
take up whole towns by the roots,
drive a piece of straw into a tree,
stick a single two-by-four into a roof
and declare it "art," stack a car
on a car on a motorcycle,
call it a night.

And that, my daughter, is how teenage boys approach love.
I don't say that it is
evil, more like an amoral force of nature,
they look all pleasant showers before they
tear your roof off and leave
your trees in shreds.
So you may dream of his blue
eyes, cloud-free compliments, the music
he likes, the motorcycle he drives,
the great tattoos on his neck, but

when the skies turn that yellow, that green,
when the hail starts popping through air

fit to boil, you listen
to my forecast, you leave the car
parked, grab a flashlight
with one hand, a blanket with the other, go
for the basement, now you run.

Pencils (At the Nebraska State Juvenile Detention Center)

They keep meticulous tabs
on the whereabouts of pencils. There are systems to it:
numbered slots in styrofoam blocks,
abbreviated haiku on the dry-erase board:

        "4 pencils
on 9–13–13
                says Miller"

and

        "10–1–13
3 pencils
                ?"

It matters. This
is a Detention Center
and a pencil

can be a Hell
of a lot more
than a pencil.

You are also told
about how necessary,
taking for granted how easy for you
to hold one, set it down wherever;

an inmate, you hear,
will break off a lead tip in class

and zip it into the lines of their palm;
in their cell, then,

they will wrap toilet paper tight
to hold the nub,
to scratch stories and poems,

small knife disappearing
into words they write.

Miles Waggener
(1970–)

Born in Phoenix, Arizona, Miles Waggener is the author of three poetry collections— Phoenix Suites *(The Word Works, 2003), winner of the Washington Prize;* Sky Harbor *(Pinyon Publishing, 2011); and* Desert Center *(forthcoming from Stephen F. Austin State University Press)—as well as two chapbooks,* Afterlives *(Finishing Line Press, 2013) and* Portents Aside *(Two Dogs Press, 2008). He has won individual artist fellowships from the Arizona Commission on the Arts and the Nebraska Arts Council. Currently, he serves as unit coordinator for the Writer's Workshop at the University of Nebraska Omaha.*

In the New Economy

You must skin the bear cub in the rain
but you lied about your credentials
and don't know how. It hangs
upside down from a tree within
eyeshot of the lodge so men who
own Taco Bells in Lubbock can
see your handiwork. The manager
who helps you hoist the animal
on Calvary, says thank god, they fly out
tomorrow, they're not paying us
by the week to drink bourbon in the
sniper's tower. You tell yourself the bear,
no bigger than a fifth-grader,
is no more like us than a dog, but
water drips from your parka onto
the dusty fur, and at its head, there's a
bright yellow bucket with rope handles you
bathe the dog in. Pine needles
stick to its muzzle. So you break the rules
and leave your post, track boot prints
across the tiles to use the off-limits
guest bathroom in the lodge, where
in a dish by the sink, there's a pile of
rosehips. *Rosa rugosa* you say
to yourself in the mirror and don't know
why you can name the sharp crowns, petals

curling into tines, regions where
masculine and feminine blur and
fall away. But you won't be seduced
by analogy. A taco mogul's bear
won't skin itself, and what they pay you for
still swings in the rain. Two of them
that day lumbered from the trees, baited
with kitchen grease, grocery store
chuck, red dye turning blue beneath the flies.
The men are loud beside the fire.
It just sat down dead, he says. I squeezed the trigger
and it sat right down. Later tonight,
you'll fry them chicken, lift them
dumplings from the broth. The mother
is still out there bleeding, they botched
the shot. Tell yourself the abattoirs
of the world are humming
without you. It'll be like
pulling a shirt the bear wore its whole life
over its head. It's nothing.
You can do this.

Moving Late at Night

The aluminum boat your father fished in, we
Had no room for it, so I said something unkind
That you repeated. Bills came and we were afraid.
Much later, when I left the motel, you told me
To just leave it, and I walked the town with the van's keys
In my hands for hours. Then sat on the edge of the bed
Like a mother talking to a feverish child
Who wasn't there: the coat, the chair where he
Read to you, his shirts in the drawer, do you
Remember when you could no longer smell him?
When there was no answer, a photograph yellowed, a face
Submerged in honey, on the cross on Indian School
Road, the overpass, where our lives detach from
Inevitability, where anything can happen then does.

Erik Campbell

(1972–)

Born in Bellevue, Nebraska, Erik Campbell's poems and essays have appeared or are forthcoming in New Letters, Tin House, Prairie Schooner, Massachusetts Review, Virginia Quarterly Review, Iowa Review, Rattle, *and other literary journals. His first poetry collection,* Arguments for Stillness *(Curbstone Press, 2006), was named by Book Sense as one of the top ten poetry collections for 2007. Red Hen Press published his second collection,* The Corpse Pose, *in June 2016. You'd like him.*

This Small Thing

I. This Small Thing

Strange to me that the nurses could shave him
but were forbidden from trimming his nails.

He was so thin by this time he looked
even more like his always thinner, paler

twin brother who, fighting the future,
never visited. Everything about him was

now small, save for his nails. His face
free of its hieroglyphics and ruddiness,

all stories and sadness bleached, smooth
as watered stone. I sat there for four hours

holding his hand, his fingernails digging
into my palm, hurting me. But he didn't

know, and hadn't known the wagging world
for days. He squeezed my hand, I hoped,

dreaming of his mother and when hers
meant warmth and unnamable things.

I couldn't know. But I remember fearing then
that the sum of us is mechanistic. That dust

makes eyes water as easily as death.
I was so eager to inhabit his hand grasping

mine with meaning, to anthropomorphize
my own father, which sounds ridiculous,

but might be what we must do. When
morphine finally loosened his grip,

I clipped his fingernails, his toenails next.
One thought only as I worked: God

damn it. And God damn it. You will not
claw your way out of this world.

II. Rooms

There will be a life
you did not choose;

it will include
many rooms.

There will be a room
you will not leave;

it will be a room
you did not choose.

III. After

Don't regret what you didn't find, a secret
diary where he unpacked his thoughts
in the private, melodic voice you always
wanted, something that might resolve
his silences, pathologize his sighs.

By now I've searched the whole house
and found only lint. But I can tell you this:

when you're later given one of his jackets,
check the pockets first. You might find

a match or a Jolly Rancher. Maybe more
lint. It matters less than little what you find,
only that you found it and don't believe it
a gift or a clue.

Faith for My Father, circa 1984

When I think about it, usually at his grave,
where I try to think funny things, faith

for my father was pragmatic in deed,
evidenced best by the night he bought

the microwave oven and made popcorn
in a bag for the first time, which was

so modern, NASA-like for my brother
and me we were suddenly science fiction,

one of the *Space Giants* or crewmembers
of Ark II. Our father squinted and jabbed

the start button, flinched slightly, retreated,
made us stand as far away from the machine

as the kitchen and Cold War would allow,
stood with arms outstretched in front of us,

Bruce Banner–style, against newly nefarious air.
And we were proud of him, would have thought

How intrepid he is, if we knew the adjectives
to fit our impossible, periodic father. Soon,

we knew, we would push past the moon; it was
what we three so wanted and tacitly wooed,

a world of unbound horizons that smelled of popcorn,
aluminum, and prescience fulfilled. "If you can

smell it," he breathed over his plaid shoulder,
"particles are escaping. So, stay behind me, for

Christ's sake." Then he lit a cigarette, inhaled and
held it, and we waited, breath bated, for the future.

Ted Genoways

(1972–)

Ted Genoways is the author of two books of poems, Bullroarer: A Sequence *(Northeastern, 2001) and* Anna, Washing *(Georgia, 2008), and two nonfiction books set in Nebraska,* The Chain: Farm, Factory, and the Fate of Our Food *(HarperCollins, 2014) and* This Blessed Earth: A Year in the Life of an American Farm *(Norton, forthcoming). He is also the editor of former Nebraska state poet William Kloefkorn's* Swallowing the Soap: New and Selected Poems *(Nebraska, 2010).*

After an Unframed Original

Big Rock, Illinois, 1941

It must be August: grandma's cotton dress
summer-sheer and sun-dappled through the trees,

grandpa's shirtsleeves rolled over his brown arms.
His hands are calloused from years on the farm,

but he lifts his son like a delicate prize,
their only child, third born, first to survive.

We had to pace down rows, reading each stone,
in the wire-fenced churchyard at the edge of town,

before we found their weathered names. Breach births,
dad explained, forced out of the womb feet first.

I only heard grandma speak of them once,
how she felt her own body clamp her son's

until she smothered him, how her daughter
cried when the cord pulled tight around her.

Two years bent by the weight of their grief,
they hold this boy, their son, light as a leaf,

and won't tell him until he's old enough
to understand that like a lantern snuffed

too quick, the frail wick of what could have been
still burns in the dark rooms inside them.

In the distance, past their tiny garden,
a farmer and his mule team are starting

across the field, making a steady rut
for seed and rain. The furrow the doctor cut

across her stomach opened wide enough
for his pink body to rise like cicadas

in the cottonwoods singing themselves free
of their husks. If not for that, I wouldn't be

whispering this in your ear, a wonder
of happenstance that brings us together,

you stranger, dear friend, whoever-you-are,
this instant caught like a snapshot or scar.

Landscape with Dust

A roiling billow, filling shadows and shafts
            of light latticed through shelterbelt trees,

ranges over corn rows and wide, dead-eyed cattle,
            a ghostly brown cloud of everywhere I've been.

It was here – Bayard, Nebraska – in this noon-heat
            shimmying off a washboard road, he saved

their town, or so I'm always told. Each day
            my grandfather turned the crank that brought

water to the valley, an orange flume that fanned
        into every field. I've heard those mud-rusted

threads squawk like an angry crow, heard
        the truck ticking in the sun, while static

cycled on the radio. Whole years pass this way,
        noon seamless into night, cicada-whirr

from the thick vines rising and falling
        like a flooded engine. But now it's a story

too often told to be true, each detail
        familiar as a leather glove that holds

the form of his hand, his fist
        white-knuckled by work, long after it is laid

on the nightstand and the man who shaped it sleeps.
        Another moon climbs in the trees, then rolls

across the blue-lit dark of another night sky.
        Day breaks with me standing in the classroom,

where my father learned to write his name,
        floorboards upturned by the trunk of a cottonwood

shouldering through the rafters and shingles
        into the open sky. It seem impossible now,

everything I've been asked to believe,
        and somewhere short miles from here

the name we share disappears from the stone.
        Then, from all stones rowed like teeth,

from this pocked blackboard, the slate
        he toted home. The letters ripple and fade

like mirages crouched at floodpoints in the road.
We speak, my family, as every family

must, in the scrawl of bloodlines, mute
tangle-vine willow tracking ancestry to a clan

of strangers. I won't look for him within
any described plot, barbed wire fencing dead

from the living. Each day the water came,
diverted by ditchwork, from somewhere

he had never been, but there it was: no miracle,
no one saved, just water to measure and dole

to farmers who paid. The day he died,
the water froze in those gutters

but when spring came the ditches ran high
with snowmelt and every mourner was out

tending his rows. I won't look for him here,
won't question anymore the silent stone,

tumbledown school, or the house crowded
now with another family I'll never know.

The script of tire tracks I leave for them in the gravel
is an heirloom for safekeeping, the cursive

of stones, the little cloud that spreads behind me
lingering barely a heartbeat in the memory

Timothy Black

(1973–)

Timothy Black's first poetic novella, Connecticut Shade*, is in its second printing through WSC Press. He teaches English and communications at Linn-Benton and Chemeketa Community Colleges and is a Cave Canem Fellow. His work has appeared in the anthologies* The Logan House Anthology of 21st Century American Poetry, The Great American Roadshow*, and* Words Like Rain. *He has been published in* Platte Valley Review *and at* bringtheink.com *and has won an Academy of American Poets prize for his poem "Heavy Freight." He lives in Albany, Oregon, with his wife and two sons.*

After Christmas Day, Evening

This water is cold enough to shatter toenails.
I caught my right foot in a fish hole
ground open by an ice auger. It is December,
and there's snow on the lake. Warm bread

on the oven back at grandmother's house.
My uncle is in the warden's shop
getting his walleye weighed.
He wants to see if it's a master.

The moon is starting to rise, and I can see it
opposite the pearlescent setting sun. My teeth
quake, and deep down I pray to feel the heat
that says it's been too long in cold water.
My uncle comes out.
When he sees me he starts to run.

What the Slaves Ate

whipcrack leather
          new shoots   a bead
momma's sore nipple
an unsupported breast
          gray goat milk
(a sonnet) for knee-deep water
(a bit) of broken tooth
(a solid chunk) of oily skin

Jones, hey blacknigger
          sing for papa   catch the glint
in his one good eye
drink this whisky bottle dry
and prepare your pleats
for another. sweaty. mouthful.

regurgitate this swallowed tooth:
          dirty river foam
          white tile roof
          a branch that can support the body's weight

(your first piece of silk)
(your first silver spoon)
(your momma's sore nipple)

          waterwalk without a ripple
          stride to where the sheerree
          wouldn't think of reaching you

Dwaine Spieker

(1974–)

Dwaine Spieker grew up on a farm outside Elgin, Nebraska, at the eastern edge of the Sandhills. Spieker's poems have appeared in numerous journals. He has published two collections, the first of which won the 2010 Nebraska Book Award. He was also a finalist for the 2014 Pablo Neruda Prize from Nimrod *and a semifinalist in 2015. Spieker lives in Wayne, Nebraska, with his wife and four children.*

County Snowplow Driver

A blade divides the white waves
south on Highway 15, and a yellow
seaworthy vessel cuts through drifts
like so much foam, its cab a sail
billowed full of coffee steam
and country music. Long before dawn
our explorer rounds Cape Horn
and sails up the Pacific Ocean
of blizzard-packed country roads.
For even a local man can know
the way Magellan must have felt,
being farther out than anyone else
yet can travel, that feeling of being
first and therefore important. Call him
adventuresome or half-crazy
or both, these roads must be opened.
Even around here we need people
willing to circumnavigate the globe
and conquer the unknown, guided
only by stars or by safety lights.

Farm-Store Advertising Flyer

Sweatshirts are on sale, flannels
and fleeces, barncoats and coveralls,
and for the first time snowboots,

a sure sign. It's late October,
the clothes have all changed colors,
and even your mailbox is a sky

you watch for signs of cold weather.
Everything portends the big change
we all know is coming, but when

is so uncertain. Even this flyer
is a paper goose, migrating through,
its wings spread wide on your table.

Benjamin Vogt

(1976–)

Benjamin Vogt was born in Oklahoma City. He received his PhD in creative writing from the University of Nebraska–Lincoln and has lived in the state since 2003. He's published three poetry collections, including Afterimage. *His poems and essays have appeared in* Creative Nonfiction, Orion, Subtropics, *and* The Sun *as well as several anthologies, including* Prairie Gold *and* The Tallgrass Prairie Reader. *Benjamin lives in Lincoln, where he writes and gardens for the Great Plains.*

Uncle with Landscape – Kansas, 1954

The corner of the farmhouse, worn by wind
that has warmed fields for centuries, is bent
and sullied to the color clouds will carry

in April. Spades and rusted buckets lean
against a toppled silo, rows of wheat –
still green like lawns – converge, a vortex

of earth that's bent, retrieved by pausing light.
A boy is standing, six or seven, hands
in overalls and hair shaved army thin.

His teeth are white as Sunday shoes,
clean arms not yet tanned by earth or grease.
His glance, below center, turns away from sun

toward ground as if the day's not possible;
that on some lost acre, black-and-white
photo in grandma's album, he's become

the lines of fields, the sway of thinning wheat,
the passing shadow, brief and cloudless night.

Last Rites

Believe me when I say that lavender cries.
This is why in autumn mornings butterflies
move silently across the stalks, buoyant
like bells that slide over altar candles.
That exhalation, after scent has ambled
toward the heavens, removes life's memory, fervent
intensity of freedom from the stem –
it makes the world a stunted requiem.
And insects burning with the forests – wings
a folded canopy of maple red,
yellow ash, umber oak – these inclined
transmuted shadows slip into this wonting.
Even we, within our lightly tended beds,
will fade into another, intertwined.

Sarah McKinstry-Brown
(1977 –)

Winner of two Nebraska Book Awards, Sarah McKinstry-Brown studied poetry at the University of New Mexico and in the University of Nebraska MFA in Writing program under Missouri's poet laureate, William Trowbridge. She's been published everywhere from West Virginia's standardized tests to literary journals such as Rattle *and* The South Dakota Review. *Born in Albuquerque, Sarah lives in Omaha with her husband, poet Matt Mason, and their two bright, feisty daughters.*

After 13 Months of Searching, the Girl's Body Is Found Five Miles from Our House

Nights we sat down to dinner, interlaced
our fingers and recited The Lord's Prayer,
she was there, taking root, a seed
with his seed inside her.

Abandoned by the sun,
lost in the thick woods
of some man's fever,
we can't stop looking at our daughters.

And when the girl's mother appears
on the evening news, distraught,
but grateful for a body, I understand.

From the deep well of our wombs,
we draw our daughters up,
bring them to our breast,
quench a thirst they didn't know
they had, saddle them with hunger
so they might stay.

Let it not be his hands that claimed her. Let it be
the tender dirt, the earth slowly awakening
to her body as it softens in the sun,
preparing her,

each pearl of larvae working to ease
the burden, to release her
from the body that caught his gaze.

Wishes

for my husband

Once, I dreamt us childless in a park in Paris.
It was a spring afternoon, and you sat
cross-legged on the grass, my head cradled
in your lap, music piped in from the heavens. I closed
my eyes to better feel the sun against my face

and awoke to you standing over me,
arms extended: *Honey,*
wake up – time to take the baby.
This is how we stumble into each
morning, fumbling

with the names our own mothers gave us.
Before this daughter,
what did we clasp our hands
and ask for, what brought us to our knees? Love

struck a match, and she appeared, little flame
whose first cry lit up every corner of this city,
before burning it
to the ground. It's raining ash, and our wishes
are so small now

we could fit them on a single candle,
hold them in the palm of our hands.

Stacey Waite
(1977–)

Born in Smithtown, New York, Stacey Waite is an assistant professor of English at the University of Nebraska–Lincoln and has published four collections of poems: Choke *(winner of the 2004 Frank O'Hara Prize),* Love Poem to Androgyny *(Main Street Rag, 2006),* the lake has no saint *(winner of the 2008 Snowbound Prize, Tupelo Press), and* Butch Geography *(Tupelo Press, 2013). Waite's poems have been published most recently in* Court Green, Pittsburgh Poetry Review, *and* Black Warrior Review.

when in summer the sound of deep rain

for maureen

the plant and its moth leaves
your grandmother's handwriting
i, in dutiful body, measure
the altar table
the neighbor cursing
with his truck and wine
the cardboard boxes he drags
to the dumpsters out back
you are drinking the red chai tea
i carry pieces of the shrine
they do not break
though i imagine them breaking

it rains all night
you sort through old clothes in the back room
i'm up collecting words
we will mostly lose
in the morning more rain
we eat bread
we remember the bodies we were

the tree is not dying
look, your friends say,
look as though we are
not tied to the ground

as though we aren't all
standing beneath the grey branches
we cannot say from here of its life
we cannot say what we might see
elsewhere
the new house lit from both sides
white pine
farmland
the trees like bridges overhead

In Nebraska

I am forced to come to terms
with the possibility of silence.
There is, in the end, something
inevitably quiet about the endless
stretch of sky, the silent vulnerability
of standing underneath it. It's hard
not to think I'm meant also to quiet down,
to shed the skin made of noise,
to pull the sound out from my throat,
let it fall silent at my feet.

"Quiet down" was what my father used to say
when we had crossed the threshold
of his short fuse. *Quiet down* as in
make your father a moment of peace
as in *leave him some room to think for once.*

But what he found when my brothers and I fell
silent in the backseat, was nothing but the open road,
nothing but the car engine – the world gone so quiet,
he could hear his eyelids touch when he blinked.

Samuel Stenger Renken

(1978–)

Samuel Stenger Renken was born in Lincoln, Nebraska, grew up in Imperial, and went to high school in Norfolk. Sam received his BA at Nebraska Wesleyan University, his MA in literature at Clemson University, and his MFA in poetry from the University of Wyoming. Sam has written poems for over two decades. His first book, Where to Start, *won the Holland Prize from Logan House Press in 2011.*

The Price of Hay's Gone Up Terribly

Van Pelt offers me a refill of coffee,
which I accept and he pours for me

while he says that two semis of hay will be in later this week
and the truckloads are getting steeper from Nebraska
hayfield to baler to loader to interstate hauler to here.
He asks how many spoons of sugar I take.

The second spoonful spills as he dumps it in,
and the white sugar salts the black rim of my mug.

The banker in him knows it,
hates it, but the worst of the herd must go
to pay for the best. He asks what I'm doing Wednesday
and if I wouldn't want to haul a stock trailer of brood mares
to meet up with a slaughter rig headed south in the afternoon.

A few drops drip on his boot
and onto the burnt sienna of the Spanish tile.
The spill washes the sugar off the rim of my mug
and leaves a ring on the table when he sets it down. I tell him I can't do it Wednes-
day and ask how many he's taking. He says, a full load of brood mares,
which I know is nine. He folds in his bottom lip to chew on it
after a sip from his cup, thinking what could've been eighteen is going to be none.

A .45 is behind glass in a red velvet shadow box
above the center window of the breakfast nook.

From this spot the horses below the hill can't see us
but they are neighing now and pawing their feeders
like they do every morning about this time.

These are the degrees of market and mammal, and
we watch the moon drop, on its full days, like a projection.
So crystalline, each crater is our lost face. The pistol
behind its glass case like a rose, oily and honed,
hangs because there's another, one that's been fired,
a smoky brother, the loaded gun under the truck seat.

Mary Hickman
(1979–)

Winner of the 2016 James Laughlin Award, Mary Hickman was born in Nampa, Idaho, grew up in China and Taiwan, and currently lives in Lincoln, where she is a visiting professor at Nebraska Wesleyan University. A graduate of the Iowa Writers' Workshop, Hickman is the author of two books of poetry, This Is the Homeland *(2015) and* Rayfish *(2017), and two chapbooks,* Ecce Animot *(2012) and* How to Be Healthy and Heal *(2011). She recently lectured and read in Turkey and Armenia as a delegate with the State Department's American Writers on Tour program.*

Geese Rising

Bring my middle to V isosceles where I become bees acting like geese's wings
really pins

And lock my waist into sky (arias!) and more silver, really chalk, that charts

Birds ascending in a V of voice where I strive to be at perfect rights with their
aerial beaks

If you will carry me, she says
If you will carry me, the geese repeat
And you should echo

Remembering Animals

1

It's like recovering
a horse from a sale.

How it feels
to lengthen, all neck. Spine
to strengthen.

2

Replanting meadow,
I listen to a Saturday track
waiting for Sunday.

3

I paint animals,
necks stretched,
heads thrown back.

I think in this one the mane
drips a black like cartographer's ink.

Ben Gotschall
(1980–)

Benjamin Gotschall was born in Atkinson, Nebraska, and grew up on a cattle ranch in the Sandhills. He earned an English degree from Nebraska Wesleyan University and a master of fine arts degree from the University of Idaho. From 2010 to 2015, he worked as an organizer to help successfully stop the TransCanada Keystone XL pipeline from crossing the Ogallala Aquifer. He now owns and operates Davey Road Ranch near Raymond, Nebraska.

Somewhere in Nebraska

I picture her horseback, one leg hooked
over the saddle horn as she watched
team roping. Hat-brim tipped
low across her eyes, she chewed sunflower-
seeds and spit the shells
at my boots. I don't remember

which rodeo, or the color
of her horse, hat, or eyes.
I'm sure the heeler caught
both feet, because when he did
she looked at me, winked, and said
Throwing a heel loop's a lot like sex –
once you get the tip in the rest is easy.

It was June or July – I forget,
but there was heat,
her unbuttoned shirt's V
and the rivulet a bead of sweat left
as it slipped along a curve of breast
when she leaned down to offer me

a handful of sunflower seeds. In my mind
her neck was tan, the shirt
sky, its buttons
pearl, but her phone number
scribbled on a rodeo-
program's torn-off corner

I can't recall. This I know: the day's heat
shaded into evening. That night
from the rise above the river, we could see
across the Sandhills. The lights
of some distant town glowed golden
like the firelight on her skin. Her hands
were small and strong, her mouth
whiskey-warm. Her hair against my face
whispered *woodsmoke, alfalfa,*
dust.

Country Wedding

for Paul and Jenn

Morning in September parts the humid
veil of summer like a breeze. Here,
in Butler County, the dragonflies must be dizzy, full
of an awareness they share with us of the coming
harvest. *Harvest,* that word at once noun and verb, both
a form of taking, and in that, taking care, in making
lists of that which will first take form
in order to be taken:
the fruit, the ears, the seed-
pods and kernels, the calves, slick and fat on grass-
milk, the hand
of a lover. Here,

somewhere between Bellwood and Ulysses, hay bales
turn their faces to the sun, the shadows of cottonwoods
tall as church steeples spread across soybeans and milo, purple tops of clover
bloom like bridesmaids, groomsmen stand in a cultivated row.
Is it foolish to think they all must carry the weight of something?
Even the ragweed we sneeze and curse will guide the wind
and hold snow to water next year's brome. So come,

let us gather around the mountain
of potato salad. Tap the cask, tune the strings,
dance like dragonflies drunk on dust. At dusk, look to the west.

When the sun sets, imagine all these things gone. Feel yourself
darken to shadow. Remember the warmth
of the day's last light, and know it is enough.

Cat Dixon

(1981–)

Cat Dixon teaches creative writing at the University of Nebraska Omaha and is the managing editor of the Backwaters Press. She is the author of Too Heavy to Carry *(Stephen F. Austin University Press, 2014),* Our End Has Brought the Spring *(Finishing Line Press, 2015), and* Eva *(Stephen F. Austin University Press, 2016). She was born on Hickam AFB in Hawaii and moved to Bellevue, Nebraska, before kindergarten. Her parents are both retired Air Force.*

For Whom the Church Doorbell Rings

You never know who will be waiting at the door, but more often than not, it's the homeless with hands held out asking for a food giftcard or anything left in the fridge. Despite being told by the minister that I shouldn't answer the door when I'm alone, I do, and then I'm rummaging for crackers in the cabinet or leftover meals. You can't say no to beggars who stream past the church in this gentrified neighborhood with its new shops and overpriced apartments. The beggars now wander past smells of baked bread from the new sandwich joint and see the snobby skinny kept women with their small dogs entering the doggie spa. So I give even when I can't or I shouldn't. One rule I held to was not to give money at the door. Like pigeons, if you throw a crust of bread, a horde will be upon you soon. The grandmother who weeps for diapers, the second request this month, who I went to Walgreens with to get the diapers last time, asks again, but I can't leave the office, so I slip into the petty cash and ask her not to tell. I bring clothes my children have outgrown, my shirts and pants I haven't worn in months, and hand them to the women who arrive begging for anything, anything. The bell is ringing like a colicky infant's cry that cannot be shushed or rocked away, so I hand over my lunch, my cash, the church cash, the water bottles saved for the youth group, the cookies in the nursery. But there is never enough. When I create a list of food pantries with dates and times to hand out, I find most visitors can't read English. It's a flood that I expect God will stop, but he doesn't. Somehow he ignores the bells and the cries and it's just me alone in the sanctuary peeking out the window to see if I should answer the door once more.

Kassandra Montag
(1987–)

Kassandra Montag was born in southern Illinois and moved to Kearney, Nebraska, when she was five. She has lived in Nebraska ever since, with the exception of a semester in Ireland and a year in the Netherlands. She holds an MA in English literature, and her writing has appeared in Prairie Schooner, Briar Cliff Review, *and* Midwestern Gothic, *among other journals. She now lives in Omaha with her husband and son.*

Flood Line

When you are gone like this,
days becoming months,
tulips blooming and then pears
growing heavy on their stems,
I find myself wanting
other men to press
their bodies against mine.

I imagine them leaning against me slightly,
in an alley stained with afternoon light,
or under the terrace of a restaurant,
cigarette smoke heavy in the air,
and then walking away
into the brown city and its fog.

I tell myself: I want them only as bodies.
But this isn't true, I want something else.
Perhaps I want desire itself,
desire a memory of the future,
remaking me in its deep sleep.

The days become cold.
A bitter wind flails from the north.
The tin wind chime on the porch
glitters with sound, the sound
of pebbles falling from a palm
on to a shore full of pebbles.

You must be in the hospital tent now,
among soldiers sitting like birds in a broken clock.
I see you holding a chart,
listening the way you listen, a waiting,
a clearing within yourself a space
for the other person.

The wind chime shakes and huddles the air.
It collides against itself, it jostles
its own corners. Its reaches
and reaches for something else.

When I was young I wanted
to be changed by choice,
not by circumstance. And now
I wonder if they are the same thing.

Before you left we walked
along the floodplain of the Missouri River.
Scouring rush tilted in the wind,
cottonwoods drooped like fallen houses.
The flood-line darkened the bottom halves
of all the trees, a mark so perfect
it made another horizon.

Kelly Weber
(1992–)

Born in Omaha, Kelly Weber grew up in St. Louis, Missouri, returning to Nebraska for high school and college. She obtained her BA in English writing and literature in 2014 and her MSE in curriculum and instruction – instructional leadership / English education in 2016, both from Wayne State College. In 2015 she served as an artist-in-residence at Cedar Point Biological Station in western Nebraska and earned the Jerry Bradley Award for Creative Writing. Her poems have appeared in Agave, Bird's Thumb, *and* Gravel.

Mentor

for JV

We talk about horses, the first
in North America before they crossed
new continents and shrugged their old selves
behind like coats, found,
butchered and eaten by a new people,
bones scraped deep.

Europeans brought their story back
shaped by wind, steppe, plain, war,
the lifting of hands and naming of earth
and ice a house, a home.
They returned in ships,
refrained across time and oceans
to the place that made them,
back toes lost and saddles added,
the bit, the bridle, the reins,
bracelets of hair, the good thing.

You love this circle.
They began here, their hooves became
their hooves, their teeth their teeth
in fold of molar, gum, crown
and they were smooth motion of wheel,
run. Before places called states
and the naming of them,

they lived, died, rode,
each day a rise
and grass, stone reaved
to high call and long spine flattened
by horizon of follow and listen, roll.

You have known this,
you have known manes and backs
and I have known mostly fear
of them, lost only slowly through touch
to equine neck and shoulders.
In this, your nearly fortieth year
of teaching those like me –
grandchildren, now, of ones you first taught
to make the fine clean line
and break and separation of poetry –
we talk horses in circles.

I've come home to these halls
to try to teach others the step,
the cautious rhythm of feet
that sent me skittering to you
so many times for help with words
in a place named for humans
on campus built mid-prairie.
Learning what shapes what
and patience of old rain.

Forgive us our silly nickering
and foolishness. We keep forgetting
what pieces of selves and bones
we've lost and gained.

For Further Reading

Poetry Anthologies
(listed chronologically)

Smith, Carl, ed. *Nebraska Poets: One Hundred Pages of Prairie Poems.* Omaha: Megeath Stationery Co., 1893.

Poets and Poetry of Nebraska: Contains Biographical Sketches and Choice Poetical Selections from the Leading Poets Now Living. Chicago: American Publishers' Assn., 1902.

Nebraska Verse, 1923–1924. Lincoln: University of Nebraska Press, 1924.

Minnesota and Nebraska Poets: An Anthology of Verse by 39 Contemporaries. New York: H. Harrison, 1937.

Humphrey, Frederick Blaine, ed. *Poems by Nebraska Poets.* 2 vols. Lincoln: The Marshall Press, 1940–41.

Kuzma, Greg, ed. *Nebraska Poets.* A special issue of *Pebble* #13. Crete, Neb.: Best Cellar Press, 1975.

———. *Forty Nebraska Poets.* Crete, Neb.: Best Cellar Press, 1981.

Sanders, Mark, ed. *The Sandhills and Other Geographies: An Anthology of Nebraska Poetry.* 2 vols. Ord, Neb.: Sandhills Press, 1980–81.

Sornberger, Judith, ed. *All My Grandmothers Could Sing: Poems by Nebraska Women.* Lincoln: Free Rein Press, 1984.

Luke, Hugh, and Hilda Raz, eds. *Nebraska: The Individual Voice.* A special issue of *Prairie Schooner* 60, no. 2 (Summer 1986).

Sanders, Mark, ed. *The Plains Sense of Things: Eight Poets from Lincoln, Nebraska.* Ord, Neb.: Sandhills Press, 1997.

———. *The Plains Sense of Things: Eight Poets from Outstate Nebraska.* Ord, Neb.: Sandhills Press, 1997.

———. *The Plains Sense of Things: A Tribute to Larry Holland.* Ord, Neb.: Sandhills Press, 1999.

Kosmicki, Greg, and Mary K. Stillwell, eds. *Nebraska Presence: An Anthology of Poetry.* Omaha: Backwaters Press, 2007.

Meats, Stephen, and Mark Sanders, eds. "Three Generations of Nebraska Poets." *Midwest Quarterly* 52, no. 4 (Summer 2011).

Hermanson, Heidi, Liz Kay, Jen Lambert, and Sarah McKinstry-Brown, eds. *The Untidy Season: An Anthology of Nebraska Women Poets.* Omaha: Backwaters Press, 2013.

Sanders, Mark, ed. *A Sandhills Reader: Thirty Years of Great Writing from the Great Plains.* Nacogdoches, Tex.: Stephen F. Austin State University Press, 2016.

Cihlar, James, and Cat Dixon, eds. *Watching the Perseids: The Backwaters Press Twentieth Anniversary Anthology.* Omaha: Backwaters Press, 2017.

Anderson, Timothy. *Lonesome Dreamer: The Life of John G. Neihardt*. Lincoln: University of Nebraska Press, 2016.

Behrendt, Stephen. "Some Preliminary Notes on Nebraska, Poetry, and Nebraska Poetry." In *Poetry from the Plains: A Nebraska Perspective*. http://poetryfromtheplains.org. 2016.

Block, Ron. "Concerning Freaks, Book Clubs, and the Unbearable Distances of the Plains." In Randolph and Shevchuk-Murray, *The Big Empty*, 2007.

Cather, Willa. "Nebraska: The End of the First Cycle." In *Roundup: A Nebraska Reader*. Ed. Virginia Faulkner. Lincoln: University of Nebraska Press, 1957.

Clark, Shelly, and Marjorie Saiser, eds. *Road Trip: Conversations with Writers*. Omaha: Backwaters Press, 2003.

Cox, Gerry, and Carol MacDaniels. *Guide to Nebraska Authors*. Lincoln: Dageforde, 1998.

Federal Writers' Project. "Literature." In *Nebraska: A Guide to the Cornhusker State*. Intro. Alan Boye. Lincoln: University of Nebraska Press, 2005.

Forsberg, Michael. *Great Plains: America's Lingering Wild*. Chicago: University of Chicago Press, 2009.

Gioia, Dana. "The Anonymity of the Regional Poet." In Sanders, *A Sandhills Reader*, 2016.

———. "The Cult of Weldon Kees." In *Weldon Kees and the Arts at Midcentury*. Ed. Daniel A. Siedell. Lincoln: University of Nebraska Press, 2003.

Hansen, Nancy Sue, and Barbara Ann Dush. *Nebraska Authors*. Vol. 1. Fullerton, Neb.: Nebraska Authors Project, 2013.

Hansen, Ron. "The Land That Time Forgot." In Randolph, *The Big Empty*, 2007.

Harvey, Alice G. *Nebraska Writers*. Rev. ed. Omaha: Citizen Print, 1964.

Hawkins, Lynn, and Muffy Fisher-Vrana. *Alive and Writing in Nebraska*. Lincoln: Media Production & Marketing, 1986.

Hickey, Donald R., Susan A. Wunder, and John R. Wunder. "Nebraska's Literary Renaissance." In *Nebraska Moments*. New ed. Lincoln: University of Nebraska Press, 2007.

Hirsch, Edward. "Nebraska Poetry." In *Poet's Choice*. Orlando: Harcourt, 2006.

Kauffman, Bernice, and Jack Brodie. *Nebraska Centennial Literary Map and Guide to Nebraska Authors*. Lincoln: Nebraska Centennial Commission in cooperation with the Nebraska Arts Council, 1967.

Kooser, Ted. *Local Wonders: Seasons in the Bohemian Alps*. Lincoln: University of Nebraska Press, 2002.

———. "Poetry." In *Encyclopedia of the Great Plains*. Ed. David J. Wishart. Lincoln: University of Nebraska Press, 2004.

Kosmicki, Greg, Lisa Sandlin, and Marjorie Saiser, eds. *Times of Sorrow, Times of Grace: Writing by Women of the Great Plains*. Omaha: Backwaters Press, 2002.

Lynch, Tom. " 'The borders between us': Loren Eiseley's Ecopoetics." In *Artifacts & Illuminations: Critical Essays on Loren Eiseley*. Ed. Tom Lynch and Susan Naramore Maher. Lincoln: University of Nebraska Press, 2012.

Maher, Susan Naramore. "Coda: Spiritual Deep Mapping and Great Plains Vernacular." In *Deep Map Country: Literary Cartography of the Great Plains*. Lincoln: University of Nebraska Press, 2014.

McCleery, David, ed. *Resource Guide to Six Nebraska Authors*. 2 vols. Lincoln: Slow Tempo Press, 1991–92.

Nebraska Voices: Telling the Stories of Our State. Lincoln: Nebraska Humanities Council, 1993.

Popper, Deborah. "Prairie Aesthetics." In *The American Midwest: An Interpretive Encyclopedia*. Ed. Richard Sisson, Christian K. Zacher, and Andrew R.L. Cayton. Bloomington: Indiana University Press, 2007.

Pratt, Linda Ray. *Great Plains Literature*. Discover the Great Plains series. Lincoln: University of Nebraska Press, 2018.

Quantic, Diane D., and P. Jane Hafen, eds. *A Great Plains Reader*. Lincoln: University of Nebraska Press, 2003.

Randolph, Ladette, ed. *A Different Plain: Contemporary Nebraska Fiction Writers*. Lincoln: University of Nebraska Press, 2004.

Randolph, Ladette, and Nina Shevchuk-Murray, eds. *The Big Empty: Contemporary Nebraska Nonfiction Writers*. Lincoln: University of Nebraska Press, 2007.

Roberts, Randy. "Margaret Haughawout." In *Lost Writers of the Plains*. http://netnebraska.org. 2015.

Sanders, Mark. "Defining the Vernacular of Nebraska Poetry." *Midwest Quarterly* 52, no. 4 (Summer 2011): 323–32.

———. "Measured Compatibility in Contemporary Nebraska Poetry: The Verse of Kloefkorn, Kooser, and Welch." *Concerning Poetry* 13, no. 2 (1980): 67–72.

———. "The Nebraska Literary Community." In *A Bibliographic Introduction to Poetry in Nebraska*. Ord, Neb.: Sandhills Press, 1992.

Sanders, Mark, and J. V. Brummels, eds. *On Common Ground: The Poetry of William Kloefkorn, Ted Kooser, Greg Kuzma, and Don Welch*. Ord, Neb.: Sandhills Press, 1983.

Stillwell, Mary K. "Being(s) in place(s): Poetry in and of Nebraska." PhD diss., University of Nebraska–Lincoln, 2004.

———. *The Life and Poetry of Ted Kooser*. Lincoln: University of Nebraska Press, 2013.

Wunder, John. "Environment and Culture." In *An Overview of the Great Plains*. Center for Great Plains Studies, University of Nebraska–Lincoln, www.unl.edu/plains/about/overview.shtml.

Organizations and Online Resources

Encyclopedia of the Great Plains. Ed. David J. Wishart. http://plainshumanities.unl.edu/encyclopedia.

Great Books of the Great Plains: Nebraska. Plains Humanities Alliance. Center for Great Plains Studies (UNL). www.unl.edu/plains/pha/phabooks.shtml.

The Jane Pope Geske Heritage Room of Nebraska Authors. Lincoln City Libraries. www.lincolnlibraries.org/heritage-room-of-nebraska-authors.

Nebraska 150 Books. Nebraska Literary Heritage Association. http://nebraska150books.org.

Nebraska 150 Celebration. https://ne150.org.

The Nebraska Center for the Book. http://centerforthebook.nebraska.gov.

Nebraska Center for Writers. Creighton University. http://mockingbird.creighton.edu/ncw.

The Nebraska Project. Straw Hat Visuals. www.nebraskaproject.com.

The Nebraska Writers Collective. http://newriters.org.

Nebraska Writers Guild. www.nebraskawriters.org.

The Nebraska Writing Project. University of Nebraska–Lincoln. www.unl.edu/newp/home.

Poetry from the Plains: A Nebraska Perspective. Department of English (UNL); Nebraska Writing Project; Center for Digital Research in Humanities. http://poetryfromtheplains.org.

Acknowledgments

Like so many good Nebraska stories, this book started out over a cup of coffee. During a visit back home in October 2015, I met Linda Ray Pratt for coffee in Omaha. Dr. Pratt had spurred my study of modern poetry with a course devoted to Yeats, Eliot, and Stevens at the University of Nebraska–Lincoln in the mid-1980s. After she told me about her new book project for the Discover the Great Plains book series that day, I wrote to her just before Thanksgiving to inquire whether anyone might be working on a Nebraska poetry anthology to celebrate the sesquicentennial. I told her that I envisioned an anthology of poets who are (or remain) active in the twenty-first century, more so than a historical anthology. In reply, she wrote: "I would like to see an anthology of Plains poetry that was historical. Who, besides Neihardt, was writing poetry in 1920 and 1930? Who wrote poetry during the late years of the nineteenth century? I don't know the answers to that, and it would require some serious research." And so, an inspiration that began thirty years ago in a classroom in Andrews Hall turned into a challenge, then a mission, and finally a far-reaching collaboration that, in a matter of months, turned into this book. It wouldn't have existed without that spark.

After some preliminary inquiries, no historical anthology seemed to be in the works, so I set about assembling *Nebraska Poetry*, knowing that if it needed to come out in spring 2017 to coincide with the statehood sesquicentennial, I had little time to waste. An initial note of inquiry to Ted Kooser led me to Mark Sanders. When I reached out to Mark at the end of November, he immediately and graciously began sharing his wealth of knowledge about Nebraska poetry, which dates to his two-volume anthology, *The Sandhills and Other Geographies* (1980–81). As a poet, scholar, and publisher of Sandhills Press, Mark has been a major shaper of the book you hold in your hands—at every step of the way, his encouragement and guidance for the project have been a beacon to me.

Ladette Randolph also provided helpful advice and moral support at an early stage. Her two edited volumes, *A Different Plain: Contemporary Nebraska Fiction Writers* (2004) and *The Big Empty: Contemporary Nebraska Nonfiction Writers* (2007), are models of judicious selection and a constant reminder of the broader literary engagements of Nebraska's poets.

Early on, I benefited from the counsel and enthusiasm of many of the poets whose work enriches these pages, especially Don Welch, Hilda Raz, Ted Kooser, Marjorie Saiser, Greg Kuzma, Stephen Behrendt, Greg Kosmicki, Twyla Hansen, Susan Aizenberg, JV Brummels, Allison Hedge Coke, Jim Cihlar, and Matt Mason. I'm grateful to all the poets who have contributed in one way or another to making this volume possible and encouraging me to see it to fruition.

To the editors of the anthologies listed in the "For Further Reading" section, my selection owes much to their own labors of love. Bookmaking, like carpentry, involves the pleasure of the well-made object, the parts of which all lend themselves to harmonious interplay. I hope the present anthology complements and honors the work of all my predecessors. Had there been fewer space and time constraints, I could have easily featured more than a hundred poets.

To Twyla Hansen, in particular, I'm indebted for her willingness, from the day we met, to champion the book even when other poet-editors with an established presence in the state would have been more obvious choices to undertake the project. Twyla's foreword provides the perfect open door to welcome readers into the anthology.

Stephen Behrendt, Linda Pratt, Mark Sanders, Ted Kooser, Mary K. Stillwell and Robert Brooke all offered welcome feedback on early drafts of my introduction.

Kimberly Verhines, director of the Stephen F. Austin State University Press, immediately signed on to publish the anthology when I broached the idea with her. SFA Press, the Backwaters Press, and Wayne State College Press continue to play an invaluable role in bringing the work of contemporary Nebraska poets to a national and international audience. My thanks to Kim and everyone at SFA Press and beyond who helped produce and promote *Nebraska Poetry*.

Numerous individuals also provided welcome assistance and encouragement along the way: Erika Hamilton, Coralie Hughes for the Neihardt Trust, Timothy Anderson, Eloise Kloefkorn (for William Kloefkorn), Dan and Eleshia Teet (for Fred Zydek), Dave McCleery (for Nancy McCleery), Teresa Ingram (for Shirley Buettner), Janet Holmes (for Susan Strayer and Mary Hickman), Kael Sagheer (for Don Welch), Denise Brady, Nancy Gillis, Joe Starita, Jeanetta Calhoun Mish, Katherine Walter, and Timothy Schaffert.

I also owe an enormous debt of gratitude to Erin Willis, curator of the Jane Pope Geske Heritage Room of Nebraska Authors at the Bennett Martin Public Library in Lincoln. Erin's immediate enthusiasm for the book, when we met with Twyla Hansen at Lincoln's Coffee House in March 2016, translated into an offer to host the formal statewide launch event as part of the John H. Ames Reading Series at the Heritage Room. In a follow-up meeting, Erin introduced me to Pat Leach, director of the Lincoln City Libraries, and Gail McNair, director of the Foundation for Lincoln City Libraries, who also provided generous and timely support for the project.

I'd also like to thank David Richards, dean of the Criss Library at the University of Nebraska Omaha, for a generous grant to defray the costs of publishing *Nebraska Poetry* and for offering to co-sponsor the Omaha launch with the UNO Writer's Workshop. Thanks as well to Denise Brady, Guy Duncan, and

Louise Duncan for producing a handsome letterpress edition showcasing ten of the women poets featured in the anthology to help celebrate the book's release.

Richard Edwards, director of the Center for Great Plains Studies at the University of Nebraska–Lincoln, also graciously offered a grant in support of the book's publication. I'm grateful to Dr. Edwards and the Center for their generous assistance.

My warm gratitude goes out to Ron Hansen, Edward Hirsch, Ted Kooser, Mary Pipher, and Marge Saiser for their glowing endorsements of the book.

Special thanks to Mike Forsberg for his inspirational cover photo, "The Gift."

My thanks as well to the Nebraska Sesquicentennial Commission for including the anthology in the Nebraska 150 Celebration, especially Regan Anson, Cynthe Johnson, and Amanda Mobley Guenther.

At the University of Oklahoma, I'm grateful to the staffs of the Western History Collections and the Bizzell Memorial Library's interlibrary loan office for providing countless rare and historic books, which proved indispensable to the timely completion of this volume.

Finally, to Aleyda. When you walked into the Hole Works in 1989, you fired my imagination with *sonetos de amor* and *canciones desesperadas*. Better than any poem on the page, you have offered me words of sunlight and shadow, plus three graces who keep me grounded as well as inspired: Cecilia, Eliana, and Sofia.

In memoriam David L. Simon (1964 – 2016)

Among what rushes will they build,
By what lake's edge or pool
Delight men's eyes when I awake some day
To find they have flown away?
– W. B. Yeats, "The Wild Swans at Coole"

Credits

All poems copyrighted by and reprinted courtesy of the authors unless otherwise noted.

Susan Aizenberg, "Meeting the Angel" and "Georgic on Waking" from *Muse* (Carbondale, Ill.: Crab Orchard Poetry Series / SIUP, 2002); "Mornings" from *Quiet City* (Kansas City, Mo.: BkMk Press, 2015).

Hartley Burr Alexander, "Pioneers!" from *Odes and Lyrics* (Boston: Marshall Jones, 1922).

Grace Bauer, "Great Plains Prayer" from *Nowhere All at Once* (Nacogdoches, Tex.: Stephen F. Austin University Press, 2014); "Note from the Imaginary Daughter" from *Retreats & Recognitions* (Sandpoint, Id.: Lost Horse Press, 2007).

Stephen Behrendt, "Coyote" from *A Step in the Dark* (Minneapolis: Mid-List Press, 1996) and "Last Leaves" from *Refractions* (Spokane, Wash.: Shechem Press, 2014).

Erin Belieu, "Plainsong" and "My Field Guide" from *One Above & One Below* (Port Townsend, Wash.: Copper Canyon, 2000).

Timothy Black, "After Christmas Day, Evening" from *Platte Valley Review*; "What the Slaves Ate" is previously unpublished.

Ron Block, "Nebraska" from *Dismal River: A Narrative Poem* (Minneapolis: New Rivers, 1990); "Salvage" from *Road Trip: Conversations with Writers*, ed. Shelly Clark and Marjorie Saiser (Omaha: Backwaters Press, 2003).

John Brehm, "Nebraska" from *december magazine;* "Valid Photo Identification Required" from *Help Is on the Way* (Madison: University of Wisconsin Press, 2012); "At the Poetry Reading" from *Sea of Faith* (Madison: University of Wisconsin Press, 2004).

JV Brummels, "Grass Widow" from *Book of Grass* (Grizzly Media, 2007); "Nevertheless New West True Gospel" from *frontpew@paradise* (Nacogdoches, Tex.: Stephen F. Austin University Press, 2017).

Clarissa Bucklin, "Inhibitions" from *Prairie Schooner* 2, no. 3 (Summer 1928), copyright © 1928 by the Wordsmiths of Sigma Upsilon; "Midwest Minerva" from *Prairie Schooner* 13, no. 1 (Spring 1939); copyright © 1939 by the University of Nebraska. Both poems reprinted by permission of the University of Nebraska Press.

Shirley Buettner, "Only the Doe Remains Voiceless," "Stillborn," and "Neighbor" from *Walking Out the Dark* (La Crosse, Wisc.: Juniper Press, 1984); "The Swiss Chalet Barometer" from *Abraxas* 25/26 (1982); "In Cottonwood Township" from *Thorns* (La Crosse, Wis : Juniper Press, 1995). Reprinted by permission of Teresa Ingram.

Lucy Martin Bullock, "Decoration Day" from *Nebraska Poets: One Hundred Pages of Prairie Poems*, ed. Carl Smith (Omaha: Megeath Stationery Co., 1893).

Kathleen Cain, "1936" from *Drought* (Uttered Chaos, Tiger's Eyes, Noah's Shoes, and Fern Rock Falls, 2016); "Sunset Clouds Rewrite History Outside Lincoln, Nebraska" from *White Pelican Review* 9, no. 1 (Spring 2008).

Erik Campbell, "This Small Thing" from *The Corpse Pose* (Pasadena, Calif.: Red Hen Press, 2016); "Faith for My Father, circa 1984" from *Nimrod International Journal* (Fall/Winter 2016).

Lenora Castillo, "La Nebraska" first appeared as "History" in a special issue on Latina/Latino literature, *Prairie Schooner* 68, no. 4 (Winter 1994), copyright © 1994 by the University of Nebraska Press. Reprinted by permission of the University of Nebraska Press.

Joy Castro, "Chicken Sandwich, Alone, Café" and "A Vertical Climb" from *Platte Valley Review* 32, no. 1 (2010–11).

Willa Cather, "Prairie Dawn" from *April Twilights (1903): Poems*, ed. Bernice Slote (Lincoln: University of Nebraska Press, 1962); "Prairie Spring" from *April Twilights and Other Poems* (New York: A. A. Knopf, 1923).

Michael Catherwood, "Balloons Drinks at the Frontier Tavern" from *Dare* (Omaha: Backwaters Press, 2006); "Projector" from *Projector* (Nacogdoches, Tex.: Stephen F. Austin State University Press, 2017).

James Cihlar, "Retrospective" from *The Threepenny Review* (Summer 2015); "Beautiful Living" from *Undoing* (Little Pear Press, 2008).

Martha Collins, "White Paper 24" from *White Papers* (Pittsburgh: University of Pittsburgh Press, 2012), © 2012 by the author and reprinted by permission of the publisher.

Orsamus Charles Dake, "Graping" from *Nebraska Legends and Poems* (Cooper Union, N.Y.: Pott & Amery, 1871).

Kwame Dawes, "Détente" from *City of Bones: A Testament* (Evanston, Ill.: Northwestern University Press, 2017). Reprinted by permission of TriQuarterly Books / Northwestern University Press.

Cat Dixon, "For Whom the Church Doorbell Rings" is previously unpublished.

Loren Eiseley, "Now the Singing Is Done" from *All the Night Wings* (New York: Times Books, 1979); "The High Plains" from *Notes of an Alchemist* (New York: Scribner's, 1972); "The Condor" from *The Innocent Assassins* (New York: Scribner's, 1973); "We Are the Scriveners" from *Another Kind of Autumn* (New York: Scribner's, 1977).

James A. Emanuel, "Negritude" and "Black Poet on the Firing Range" from *Whole Grain: Collected Poems, 1958–1989* (Detroit: Lotus Press, 1991). Reprinted by permission of Broadside Lotus Press.

Gene Fendt, "*Magister verborum*" is previously unpublished.

Charles Fort, "We Did Not Fear the Father" from *The Georgia Review* (Summer 1999); "The Vagrant Hours" from *The Best American Poetry 2003*, ed. Yusef Komunyakaa (New York: Scribner Poetry, 2003). Both poems appear in *We Did Not Fear the Father: New and Selected Poems* (Pasadena, Calif.: Red Hen Press, 2012).

Ione Gardner, "I Have Put Away All Things" and "Tall Girl" from *Nebraska Verse, 1923–1924* (Lincoln: University of Nebraska Press, 1924).

Ted Genoways, "After an Unframed Original" from *Southern Review* 38, no. 3 (Summer 2002); "Landscape with Dust" from *Bullroarer* (Boston: Northeastern University Press, 2001).

Ben Gotschall, "Somewhere in Nebraska" from *Where It Happened* (Scotia, Neb.: Sandhills Press, 2008); "Country Wedding" is previously unpublished.

Twyla M. Hansen, "We Are on Nine-Mile Prairie When" from *Potato Soup* (Omaha: Backwaters Press, 2003); "After a Rain" and "August 12 in the Nebraska Sand Hills Watching the Perseids Meteor Shower" from *Dirt Songs: A Plains Duet* (Omaha: Backwaters Press, 2011); "Sandhill Cranes" from *Rock • Tree • Bird* (Omaha: Backwaters Press, 2017).

Neil Harrison, "Spring Burial in the Sandhills" from *Clover*, vol. 4; "This Bike Path Now Called the Cowboy Trail" from *Nebraska Life* (November/December 2014).

Margaret Haughawout, "Foiled," "Ruthless," "To a Good Girl," "At a Teachers College," and "A Learned Lady" from *Sheep's Clothing* (Pittsburg, Kan.: n.p., 1929).

Allison Hedge Coke, "Waiting for Light" and "Then" from *Streaming* (Minneapolis: Coffee House Press, 2014).

Mary Hickman, "Geese Rising" and "Remembering Animals" from *This Is the Homeland* (Boise, Id.: Ahsahta Press, 2015), reprinted by permission of Ahsahta Press.

Larry Holland, "Home School" and "The Whisper of Bones Grating" from *Disciples of an Uncertain Season* (Winside, Neb.: Logan House, 2001). Copyright 2001 by the Estate of Larry Holland. Reprinted by permission of the publisher.

Art Homer, "Turkey Vultures" and "Five A.M., That Small Problem Again" from *Blind Uncle Night* (Cincinnati, Ohio: WordTech Press, 2014).

Lavon Jarvis, "No Cathedral" and "Spring Returns to the Prairie" from Harrison, *Minnesota and Nebraska Poets,* 1937.

Weldon Kees, "For My Daughter," "Dynamite for Operas," "Poem Instead of a Letter," "1926," and "Small Prayer" from *The Collected Poems of Weldon Kees*, ed. Donald Justice, 3rd ed. (Lincoln: University of Nebraska Press, 2003). Copyright © by the estate of Weldon Kees. Reprinted by permission of the Jane Pope Geske Heritage Room of Nebraska Authors, Lincoln City Libraries, Lincoln, Nebraska.

William Kloefkorn, "Out-and-Down Pattern" and "My Love for All Things Warm and Breathing" from *Cottonwood County* (Lincoln, Neb.: Windflower Press, 1979); "At Bryan LGH–East in Lincoln, Nebraska" and "My Granddaughter, Alyssa" from *Midwest Quarterly* 52, no. 4 (Summer 2011). Reprinted by permission of Eloise Kloefkorn.

Ted Kooser, "Etude" from *Weather Central* (Pittsburgh: University of Pittsburgh Press, 1994), © 1994 by the author and reprinted by permission of the publisher; "Screech Owl" and "Pearl" from *Delights & Shadows* (Port Townsend, Wash.: Copper Canyon Press, 2004); "Sleep Apnea" from *Splitting an Order* (Port Townsend, Wash.: Copper Canyon Press, 2015).

Greg Kosmicki, "My Flag" from *when there wasn't any war* (Omaha: Backwaters Press, 1987); "Deodorant" and "Sitting in a Concrete Parking Garage" from *New Route in the Dream* (Columbus, Ohio: Pudding House, 2011).

Greg Kuzma, "The Tree," "An August Evening," and "The Birds My Son Showed Me" from *Hose and Iron* (Nacogdoches, Tex.: Stephen F. Austin State University Press, 2016).

Steve Langan, "Prairie Poem with Lines from Emily Dickinson" from *Make* 7 (Fall 2008/Winter 2009); "The Book Finally with All the Misery in It" from *Meet Me at the Happy Bar* (Buffalo, N.Y.: BlazeVOX, 2009).

Glenna Luschei, "Startled to Wake" from *The Sky Is Shooting Blue Arrows* (Albuquerque: University of New Mexico Press, 2014).

Kelly Madigan, "Reliquary" from *Best New Poets 2007*, ed. Natasha D. Trethewey and Jeb Livingood (Charlottesville, Va.: Samovar Press, 2007); "Nebraska" from *Massachusetts Review* (Winter 2004–2005), reprinted in *The Edge of Known Things* (Nacogdoches, Tex.: Stephen F. Austin State University Press, 2013).

Helene Magaret, "Song of the Answerer," "Prairie Women," "In Answer to a Letter," and "Come Out of the Cold" from *Change of Season: Lyrics* (New York: Farrar & Rinehart, 1941).

Matt Mason, "Notes for My Daughter Against Chasing Storms" from *The Baby That Ate Cincinnati* (Nacogdoches, Tex.: Stephen F. Austin University Press, 2013); "Pencils (At the Nebraska State Juvenile Detention Center)" is previously unpublished.

Nancy McCleery, "Everything Keeps Me Here, the Swallow" and "Family on the Platte" from *Staying the Winter* (Omaha: The Cummington Press, 1987); "Girl Talk (music / purity)" from *Girl Talk* (Omaha: Backwaters Press, 2002).

R. F. McEwen, "Stacking Rick Wood: Getting On" from *Casey Joe MacBride's White River: Vol. 1* (Nacogdoches, Tex.: Stephen F. Austin University Press, 2014); "John Early Remembers the Moment of His Wife's Death" from *Prairie Schooner* 80, no. 1 (Spring 2006), copyright © 2006 by the University of Nebraska Press. Reprinted by permission of the University of Nebraska Press.

Sarah McKinstry-Brown, "After 13 Months of Searching, the Girl's Body Is Found Five Miles from Our House" and "Wishes" from *Cradling Monsoons* (Fairfield, Iowa: Blue Light Press, 2010).

Kassandra Montag, "Flood Line" is previously unpublished.

John G. Neihardt, "If This Be Sin," "Easter," and excerpt from *The Death of Crazy Horse* from *Lyric and Dramatic Poems* (Lincoln: University of Nebraska Press, 1965). Copyright © 1954 by John G. Neihardt. Reprinted by permission of the Neihardt Trust.

Tillie Olsen, "I Want You Women up North to Know" (1934) from *Tell Me a Riddle, Requa I, and Other Works* (Lincoln: University of Nebraska Press, 2013) by permission of the University of Nebraska Press and the Frances Goldin Literary Agency. Copyright © 2013 by the Board of Regents of the University of Nebraska.

Edwin Ford Piper, "Dry Bones" from *Barbed Wire and Wayfarers* (New York: Macmillan, 1924), "Big Swimming," "Indian Counsel," "You Too," and "In Dust and Gilt" from *Paintrock Road* (New York: Macmillan, 1927).

Amy Plettner, "Letter to Paul in Prison" from *Undoing Orion's Belt* (Wayne, Neb.: WSC Press, 2011); "Church Bulletin" from *Rattle* (Summer 2014).

Hilda Raz, "Diction" from *The Bone Dish* (Brockport, N.Y.: State Street Press, 1989); "Fast Car on Nebraska I-80: Visiting Teacher" and "Prelude" from *TRANS* (Middletown, Conn.: Wesleyan University Press, 2001).

Samuel Stenger Renken, "The Price of Hay's Gone Up Terribly" from *Where to Start* (Wayne, Neb.: Logan House, 2011).

Marjorie Saiser, "Luke Says It's Another Silly Idea" from *Losing the Ring in the River,* copyright © 2013 by the University of New Mexico Press, reprinted by permission of the publisher; "Pulling Up Beside My Husband at the Stoplight" from *Beside You at the Stoplight* (Omaha: Backwaters Press, 2010); "The Story, Part of It" from *I Have Nothing to Say about Fire* (Backwaters, 2016); "Father" from *Lost in Seward County* (Omaha: Backwaters Press, 2001).

Mark Sanders, "Plain Sense," "On Horseback, Hell's Gate Canyon, October," and "The Cannas" from *Conditions of Grace: New and Selected Poems* (Nacogdoches, Tex.: Stephen F. Austin State University Press, 2011).

Roy Scheele, "Tell Me Again" and "Home Stretch" are previously unpublished.

Barbara Schmitz, "Supper" and "I Go to Hell" from *How to Get Out of the Body* (Grand Island, Neb. / Pearland, Tex.: Sandhills Press, 1999).

Karl Shapiro, excerpt from *The Bourgeois Poet* and "Western Town" from *Collected Poems, 1940–1978* (New York: Random House, 1978). Reprinted by permission of Harold Ober Associates.

Daniel Simon, "Cast Off" and "Portrait in 2/4" from *Cast Off* (McRae, Ark.: Edwin Smith, 2015).

Michael Skau, "Cranes" and "Freedom's Slaves" are previously unpublished.

Bernice Slote, "Grandfather" from *Prairie Schooner* 21, no. 2 (Summer 1947), copyright © 1947 by the University of Nebraska Press. Reprinted by permission of the University of Nebraska Press.

Judith Sornberger, "My Twin Sons Talk with Me about Survival" from *Open Heart* (Corvallis, Ore.: Calyx Books, 1993); "Wal-Mart Orchid" from *Wal-Mart Orchid* (Columbus, Ohio: Evening Street Press, 2011).

Marcia Southwick, "Small Difficulties" and "The Ruins" from *Why the River Disappears* (Pittsburgh: Carnegie Mellon University Press, 1990).

Dwaine Spieker, "County Snowplow Driver" from *Nebraska Life Magazine* (January/February 2013); "Farm-Store Advertising Flyer" from *Nimrod* (Fall/Winter 2014).

Mary K. Stillwell, "A Waltz for My Mother" and "The Cutting" from *Maps & Destinations: New and Selected Poems* (Nacogdoches, Tex.: Stephen F. Austin University Press, 2014).

Susan Strayer Deal, "Elegy" from Sanders, *The Sandhills and Other Geographies*, vol. 1; "Distant Cousins" from *The Dark Is a Door* (Boise, Idaho: Ahsahta Press, 1984), reprinted by permission of Ahsahta Press.

Terese Svoboda, "Sex and Class and Race," "The Ranchhand's Daughter," and "Sylph" from *When the Next Big War Blows Down the Valley: Selected and New Poems, 1985–2015* (Tallahassee, Fla.: Anhinga Press, 2015).

Laura Tohe, "The Platte / Platte Tooh Nílínígíí" from *Making Friends with Water* (Omaha: Nosila Press, 1986).

William Trowbridge, "Stark Weather" from *Put This On, Please: New and Selected Poems* (Pasadena, Calif.: Red Hen Press, 2014); "Peony Park, Omaha" from *Burnt District* (Summer 2015).

John Trudell, "Crazy Horse" and "Cry Your Tears" from *Lines from a Mined Mind* (Golden, Colo.: Fulcrum, 2008). Copyright © 2008 by John Trudell. Reprinted by permission of Fulcrum Publishing, Inc.

Benjamin Vogt, "Uncle with Landscape – Kansas, 1954" and "Last Rites" from *Afterimage* (Nacogdoches, Tex.: Stephen F. Austin University Press, 2012).

Miles Waggener, "In the New Economy" from *River Styx* 87 (May 2012); "Moving Late at Night" from *North American Review* 300, no. 3 (Summer 2015).

Stacey Waite, "when in summer the sound of deep rain" from *Hoppenthaler's Congeries* 5, no. 7 (May 2016), www.connotationpress.com; "In Nebraska" is previously unpublished.

Kelly Weber, "Mentor" is previously unpublished.

Don Welch, "Nebraska" from *The Rarer Game* (Kearney, Neb.: Kearney State College Press, 1980); "When Memory Gives Dust a Face" and "Requiem for a Teacher" from *When Memory Gives Dust a Face* (Lewiston, Idaho: Lewis-Clark Press, 2008); "When That Snow Died" from *Travels* (Georgetown, Ky.: Finishing Lines Press, 2010).

Kathleene West, "For a Long Winter" from *Water Witching* (Port Townsend, Wash.: Copper Canyon, 1984); "Plain Talk from the Platte River" and "Farm Wife" from *Plainswoman: Her First Hundred Years* (Ord, Neb.: Sandhills Press, 1985), "Progression" from *The Farmer's Daughter* (Ord, Neb.: Sandhills Press, 1988). Reprinted by permission of Mark Sanders.

Donna Whitewing-Vandall, "Love Song" from *The Whispering Wind: Poetry by Young American Indians*, ed. Terry Allen (Garden City, N.Y.: Doubleday, 1972); "August 24, 1963—1:00 A.M.—Omaha" from *Voices from Wah'Kon-Tah: Contemporary Poetry of Native Americans*, ed. Robert K. Dodge and Joseph B. McCullough (New York: International Publishers, 1974); "[Untitled]" from *Four* (Santa Fe, N.M.: Institute of American Indian Arts, 1965).

Fredrick Zydek, "Nebraska Quartet" from *At the Edge of the Ancient Inland Sea: Poems from the Nebraska Experience* (Omaha: Backwaters Press, 2012); "Star Watching" from *Stumbling Through the Stars: New Poems* (Omaha: Holmes House, 2004).

Index